"Being Down"

"Being Down"

CHALLENGING VIOLENCE
IN URBAN SCHOOLS

Ronnie Casella

Foreword by Jean Anyon

Teachers College, Columbia University
New York and London

Published by Teachers College Press, 1234 Amsterdam Avenue, New York, NY 10027

Library of Congress Cataloging-in-Publication Data

Casella, Ronnie, 1963–
    "Being down" : challenging violence in urban schools / Ronnie Casella ; foreword by Jean Anyon.
        p. cm.
    Includes bibliographical references (p.) and index.
    ISBN 0-8077-4148-5 (cloth : alk. paper) — ISBN 0-8077-4147-7 (pbk. : alk. paper)
    1. School violence—United States—Prevention—Case studies. 2. Education, Urban—Social aspects—United States—Case studies. 3. Socially handicapped teenagers—Education—United States—Case studies. I. Title: Challenging violence in urban schools. II. Title.

LB3013.32 .C37 2001
373.17′82—dc21   2001027730

ISBN 0-8077-4147-7 (paper)
ISBN 0-8077-4148-5 (cloth)

Printed on acid-free paper

Manufactured in the United States of America

08 07 06 05 04 03 02 01   8 7 6 5 4 3 2 1

Contents

Foreword

Before analyzing a phenomenon, a researcher must lay a foundation with a basic premise. Most current literature on school violence assumes that the issue arises primarily because of the behavioral problems of young people, and addressing these will alleviate the trouble across the country. In *"Being Down"*, however, Ronnie Casella shows how school violence is not only a product of teenage anger and alienation but also of a host of social problems. This insightful study examines the way violence is constructed through social policy and popular rhetoric. In his view, then, the roots of violence in city schools can be traced to a large extent to social forces and inequities on a broad scale, and, closer to home, to neighborhood violence and the surrounding distressed urban environment.

Casella concludes that the sustainability of successful violence prevention in schools depends on the degree to which it connects with the establishment of environmental, racial, and economic justice. He argues that we cannot absolve society by blaming violence in schools on teachers, students, administrators, or even families. Such violence is also caused by social phenomena like stark inequality and lack of economic and political access.

Casella's book is right on target. In violence prevention, as with so many other educational problems, social policies must supplement educational policies in our search for viable solutions. Ronnie Casella demonstrates that it is up to all of us to work together to rid society of the underlying causes of rage and violence in America, and thus make our schools safer. *Being Down* is a much needed work which encourages us to look at school violence in this broader perspective.

Jean Anyon

Acknowledgments

Though a rather solitary pursuit, the writing of this book was not an individual endeavor. There were people who made the research possible and who helped to improve the writing. From the very beginning, the administration at Brandon High let me join them as they went about the business of running a school. If I was a nuisance, as I am sure I was at times, they nevertheless permitted me to attend meetings and classes, to have free access to most aspects of the school, and to question them endlessly. A counselor, two assistant principals, the principal, the coordinator of the afternoon school program, the social worker, and several parents were especially accommodating. Two social studies teachers and several health teachers opened their classroom doors to me. All took time out of their busy schedules to be interviewed, sometimes several times during the year, and their insights ripple throughout this book.

I reserve heartfelt thanks for the students who allowed me to interview them, to attend their classes, and to chat with them after school and during their free periods. There were many students I met who had little reason to trust an adult they did not know well. Yet many took time to teach me about the school, their city, and the violence in their lives.

There were staff at several community and nonprofit groups in the city, and directors of programs, who gave their time to meet with me and kept me informed of city and community meetings, which I then attended. Through these meetings, I met many people who gave freely of their time and ideas, and who provided important information about violence-prevention efforts in the city and its schools.

The city police department allowed me to interview officers and to spend a year with one of their school police officers. Several officers took me around Brandon city on their beats, allowed me to interview them, and kept me informed about crime in the city. The school police officer, who was a detective in the city police department, seemed to always have time for the work I was doing. The DARE (Drug Abuse Resistance Education) teacher permitted me to sit in on his classes and shared student evaluations of the program. The school guards let me spend much time with them as they patrolled the school, and though some seemed to enjoy the company, I learned much from them and no doubt gained from these experiences more than they did.

The research itself was supported by the Office of Juvenile Justice and Delinquency Prevention through the Hamilton Fish National Institute on School and Community Violence at George Washington University and the Violence Prevention Project at Syracuse University. Sincere thanks to Joan Burstyn, co-Principal Investigator of the Violence Prevention Project at Syracuse University, for the opportunity to conduct the research and for providing crucial insights about the work we were doing. Kim Williams and Rebecca Stevens gave feedback in weekly meetings where we discussed our efforts as part of the Violence Prevention Project. Meetings can be the bane of university life, but these were always inspiring and well worth the countless hours we spent discussing data and the research program.

There were several people whose comments about the writing in this book pushed me to better construct my arguments. Maureen Gilroy helped me to develop my ideas and characterizations of students. Robert Bogdan, with his keen eye for the "big picture" of a book, urged me to link my writing to concepts by authors who have addressed similar topics. Sari Knopp Biklen, a wonderful cultural analyst, provided feedback that helped me to better develop arguments in several chapters of the book. Diane Pollard and Ellen Brantlinger were especially insightful in their feedback on the initial draft of the book. In addition, the reviewers and staff at Teachers College Press helped me throughout all stages of the project and were particularly rigorous with their work. Sincere thanks to all.

"Being Down"

Introduction

During my research for this book, a school police officer told me, "When I was in school and I had a problem with a kid, at worst we'd meet outside and have it out with our fists. Now when kids have a problem they meet in the hallways and have it out with their guns and knives." For many, it seems, there was a Golden Age—a time when life was simpler; when worries about security and safety were not so severe; when, in fact, schools did not need police officers.

Now, of course, police officers in schools are more often than not the norm. This book investigates why that is the case; what societal, economic, and historical factors have created such a situation; and how the situation is linked to new crime policy and the realities of urban and youth violence. There are three interrelated aspects of school violence that are discussed: the role of violence in the lives of students; the construction of violence in policy and popular rhetoric; and the way violence is enacted by schools through disciplinary policies and policing strategies. These three aspects of violence direct attention not only to the adolescents who sometimes act violently but also to the influence that public discussions and policies have in forming understandings and responses to the problem. *"Being Down"* brings to the fore the consequences students face when they attend schools that have always been and remain nearly as violent as the communities in which they are set. It also views violence as an outcome not only of personal interactions, but also of interactions among individuals and school systems.

When it comes to school violence, the Golden Age story is a sleight-of-hand trick, a way of slicing off one sliver of history from the rest. In the United States, connections between aggression and schooling have a long and varied history that includes not only incidents of violence but also expectations that schooling would enforce a moral code and be an agent of stability that would prevent delinquency even outside of school (Adams, 1988; Tyack, 1974; Tyack & Cuban, 1995). Regarding youth, we have years of research—traceable to Frederic Thrasher's sociological study *The Gang* (1927) and Clifford Shaw's *The Jack-Roller* (1930/1966)—that have

1

linked violence to the permanence of poverty, youth alienation, educational failure, and structural constraints in U.S. society. Newer literature and concerns have been directed at middle-class and seemingly stable white children, including girls (Artz, 1998; Garbarino, 1999; Kivel, 1999; Perlstein, 1998; Pollack, 1999).

In this literature, there seems to be a growing sense that there are "brands" of violence—black, urban, and gang violence on one end of the spectrum; white, suburban, and media violence on the other. This bifurcation assumes not only rather simple brands of violence but also simple brands of people and places. The focus of this book is a school in a city that is diverse racially, economically, and in lifestyle—a city surrounded by working-class and wealthy suburbs and within two miles of farmland. It is a city where suburban-like streets exist only a few blocks from downtown, where a prestigious medical center and university stand side-by-side with housing projects and gangland. The school that we get to know is populated with a diversity of people of different social classes, experiences, and attitudes—a place where staff must deal with the down-side of urban loss and poverty, as well as middle-class mobilities, demands, and insecurities. It is a school that belies some of the narrow thinking that has defined and boxed in ideas about "urban violence," "school violence," "gang violence," and other such *brands*.

In Chapter 1, I make the point that school violence is more than acts of violence in school. It is fashioned in policy and rhetoric as part of a larger problem with youth, discipline, and schools. In his book about the panic that swept through the 1980s regarding child abuse and disappearances, Joel Best (1990, p. 177) made the point that the "missing-children problem" was as much a scare that gained unprecedented national attention in the "social problem marketplace" of the 1980s as a problem involving truly abused and threatened children. In addition to ongoing acts of abuse, a slew of events converged that created greater awareness and sometimes panic around the problem. These included social policy (Child Abuse Victims' Rights Act of 1986 and Child Sexual Abuse and Pornography Act of 1986); public service campaigns (photographs of missing children on milk cartons); publicized accounts and frights (spiked Halloween candy, random abductions); and the incorporation of the theme in popular culture (the bestselling book *It* by Stephen King, most slasher films).

School violence at the start of the 21st century is like the missing-children problem of the 1980s. It has won out in the social problem marketplace. Many more young people are killed in urban streets, shoot themselves, or are shot by accident than are killed in schools, but the focus on gun violence has been set largely in the schools (see Elliott, Hamburg, & Williams, 1998; Hyman & Snook, 1999; McCord, 1997). A variety of interests (including greater numbers of middle-class and white students shooting and killing each other in schools), national policies through most of the 1990s (Gun-Free School Zones Act of 1990 and Safe Schools Act of 1994), and severe tragedies of violence have converged to create greater awareness about a problem that is far from new.

In no way do I want to skirt the reality of violence and its devastating consequences on people's lives, but neither do I want to cut off the public response from the problem itself. Howard Becker's conclusions in *Outsiders* remain true today (1963, p. 14): "Deviance is not a quality that lies in behavior itself, but in the interaction between the person who commits an act and those who respond to it." Entwined in the brutality and suffering caused by violence are assumptions that shape reactions to the problem— reactions that can, at times, exacerbate the problem.

David Anderson (1998, p. 328) pointed out that for school staff, increases in violence are often more qualitative than quantitative and involve issues not always revealed in the compilation of incident statistics. In Chapter 2, I examine this point by highlighting the words of students and teachers and by presenting descriptions of life in school. The chapter discusses violence in several ways: not only as weapon violence, but also as fighting, as forms of harassment and abuse, as threats and bullying, and as suicide. In general, my own definition follows that of the National Center for Education Statistics [NCES] (1995, 1998) and the National Institute of Justice [NIJ] (1995), but it also aims to account for school violence in the context of the city, within the realities of prejudice and poverty, and in reference to discipline policy, and especially zero tolerance.

The book makes the point that what is called "school discipline" is too often a means of "outplacing" students with severe problems. This is done by either prodding them to drop out through suspension or expulsion, or by transferring them to a kind of alternative school, boot camp, or detention center, set up for their isolation. Who is going to listen to such kids when already they are thought of as beyond help and almost naturally on their way to lives of crime? These general feelings, described in Chapter 3, are accompanied by unfair punishments, educational failures, and an almost inconceivable set of school ironies. Among those ironies are the following: The only way for a school to deal with a troubled kid is to give her more trouble. The only way to deal with a kid who does not want to be in school is to kick him out. As this book points out, this kind of doublethink becomes naturalized; it is called "discipline policy" and then seen as the only way to deal with kids who have ruined, for some adults, a Golden Age that never really existed.

The disciplinary role of schooling is followed up on in Chapters 4, 5, and 6 by focusing on policing efforts in the city and the school. In the first two of these chapters, I draw on observations of police officers, combined with interviews with them, to examine the animosities, and sometimes unexpected alliances, that develop among police officers and city kids and their families. In the discussion about the Drug Abuse Resistance Education (DARE) program in Chapter 6, I reexamine issues raised about school policing, this time from the perspective of pedagogy and in relation to classroom dynamics. In each of these chapters, I study violence within the context of what Jeffrey Fagan and Deanna Wilkinson (1998, p. 81) saw as the interaction of "individual developmental needs and goals" within "social and structural contexts of neighborhoods and communities." The chapters show how race, power struggles, gender, academic standing in the school, social class, and neighborhood all play a part in creating impressions about violence, schooling, and youth. These impressions, in turn, not only shape policy but also influence relationships among youth, police officers, and school staff.

Essentially, part of what I demonstrate in this book is that school violence is not only a behavioral problem but also a public production that steers the formation and implementation of policy, shifts blame away from middle-class and adult society, denigrates public schools, and offers excuses for a multitude of social problems. Too often, understandings about school violence are constrained by a narrow view of the problem. In some research and in most popular rhetoric, individuals pinpoint media, poverty, prejudice, alienation, immorality, hormones, and a host of "lacks" (lack of religion, lack of parental involvement, lack of discipline) as the *root causes* of violence, but rarely view the problem from a perspective that would account for each situation when necessary and reject those that are not pertinent in particular cases.

In addition to behavior, school violence is enacted within a context of school hierarchies, policies and reforms, social interactions, and disciplinary practices. Ironically, the point of this book is to say the obvious: All of society is responsible for a public system (such as a school) that is violent. We all contribute to it and we all harbor the power to do something about it. The means of reform, and how this reform must take into consideration the behavior of students, the realities of their neighborhoods, the sometimes oppressive environments of schools, and enactments of power along socioeconomic, gender, and racial lines, is the focus of the last chapter.

SCHOOL VIOLENCE AT GROUND LEVEL

Students go to school (one hopes) with pencils and papers in hand. And so did I, though I used them for different reasons. I recorded events that took place in school and interviewed those who would speak to me. I spent many hours each week talking to students, administrators, school and city police, teachers, and community organizers; I observed violence-prevention programs, including peer mediation and DARE classes; and I traveled with police officers on their beats in school and in the city as school let out. In short, I examined school violence from ground level. I focused on the nature of violence in school, on forms of discipline policy, and on prevention and policing strategies used to curb violence. My attention was on violence *in* school but also on the school *within* the city and youth *within* popular rhetoric and policies regarding schooling and violence in U.S. society.

The school-based research was conducted from August 1997 to July 1998 and was funded by the Office of Juvenile Justice and Delinquency Prevention, under the auspices of the Hamilton Fish National Institute on School and Community Violence at George Washington University and the Violence Prevention Project at Syracuse University. It was initiated with participant observations in a high school, which I call Brandon High, in New York State, and in the city around the school, which I refer to as Brandon city (see also Biklen, 1995; Fordham, 1996; McQuillan, 1998). All names of individuals, schools, and organizations mentioned in this book are pseudonyms. Also included as data were school and central office documents and reports, and booklets, handouts, and articles about violence distributed by the school and community groups.

In 1999–2000, I continued research on school violence in another urban high school in a neighboring state. The research reported here is part of a larger study that has included research in other schools and in a prison. While I do not include data from the larger study, my conclusions here have been colored by this other research. The themes developed in this book have resurfaced again and again, though sometimes in different ways, and I have seen that while my conclusions and observations in this book do not hold true for all schools in all areas, neither am I dealing with unique and distinct circumstances and issues.

Most interviews with adults were tape-recorded and transcribed. Others were not recorded but transcripts were written based on my notes taken during the interviews. Most of what I learned from adults and students came from conversations in informal settings—in the hallway of the school, in the cafeteria, outside during lunch. During observations, I took copious field notes and also transcribed them. These field notes and interview transcripts were coded, and the codes were then condensed according to themes. Hypotheses were inductively generated, in the fashion of grounded theory, and conclusions were made "from the bottom up" and "from many disparate pieces of collected evidence that are interconnected" (Bogdan & Biklen, 1998, p. 6; see also Athens, 1997; Erickson, 1973).

Basic to the research is the belief that people make meaning of the world through a symbolic interpretation of what they see, hear, and feel but that school violence is also more than "symbolic" (Blumer, 1969; Denzin, 1992; Lincoln, 1988).

A BIRD'S-EYE VIEW OF VIOLENCE

Decades ago, at a time when the United States had taken on the challenge to declare a war on poverty, Elliot Liebow's *Tally's Corner* (1967) made the still timely point that life's circumstances are always connected to issues that extend beyond individual flaws and choices that people make. Though the topics differ, his conclusions about the black men he studied in a blighted Washington, D.C., neighborhood make sense for what I have come to see in the lives of many students, for whom violence seems eternally connected to issues involving respect, prejudice, sex, property, power, and convoluted histories of their families, friends, and neighborhoods. As with the men in Liebow's study, the students' problems are both cultural and structural (see Casella, 1999; Feuerverger, 1998; Levinson & Holland, 1996, p. 14).

School and youth violence are also an "integral part of the larger society," to quote Liebow (p. 209). But things have changed since the 1960s when such structural perspectives began to take root. Then, in spite of their limitations, there were national reform efforts that attempted to help the poor through public assistance—there were the "blue welfare checks" that Liebow described. Now, we have "welfare role cuts." The reforms of the 1960s have given way to "get tough" policies and cutting back on Great Society safety nets and ideals. To be blunt, the structure is different today and people skirting the margins of society face a judicial system that has swallowed up progressive attempts at rehabilitation and hope.

The more cultural-ecological approach to delinquency that is used in this book has its roots in Chicago School sociology and the early studies of delinquency by Clifford Shaw (1930/1966) and Frederick Thrasher (1927), mentioned earlier. The ecological approach taken by Richard Cloward and Lloyd Ohlin in *Delinquency and Opportunity* (1960, p. 86) made the point that violence was sometimes the outcome of anomie or a general breakdown in society. Drawing from the work of Emile Durkheim and Robert Merton, they explained that "lower-class youth are led to want and what is actually available to them is the source of a major problem . . . and intense frustration" that may lead to violence.

A common thread running through this perspective is that youth are socially and economically isolated—that they have conventional wants but opportunities are not there that enable them to obtain what most middle-class people have. This perspective directs attention to the way individuals and social structures at times interact to create violent situations, for example, the way poverty influences cultural values, or the way that economically oppressed youth demand interpersonal respect from peers in ways that so often lead to battles. But as mentioned earlier, though I draw from this perspective, the world is different today and youth face challenges from schools, police forces, and the criminal justice system that until recently were not so pronounced.

These challenges—in this newer world—are presented in this book. One thing that should be noticed is that urban areas are not distinct territories unto themselves. They are not as "socially isolated" as many have represented them to be—even our most *inner* "inner cities" have been stamped with various kinds of urban policies, have undergone stages of gentrification and real estate development, and are always in flux and connection with the political and economic world beyond the heart of the ghetto.

This is not to say that ghettos do not exist, or that they do not deal with unique problems and circumstances; rather, it is to say that sometimes there is the belief that urban youth act violently because they are cut off from the mainstream world. They are outside its laws, values, and the places where opportunities abound and money is made. But beyond the economic pressures and isolation bearing down on the "urban enclave" or "ghetto" or "inner city" are the middle-class institutions, schools, social services, courts, and prisons that draw even the most socially isolated individuals into the professional, middle-class world. Contrary to some studies of youth and school violence, youth act violently not only because of their social isolation but also because of their contact and misfortunes with the professional systems that have been set up apparently to help them.

CHAPTER 1

A Framework for Understanding Violence in School

In the United States there has often been a strong "banging at the door" feeling about violence. Violence is seen as something evil and foreign existing on the outside that intends to invade middle- and upper-class properties, comfort, security, and institutions. In schools, the "violence at our door" mentality has led to the installment of metal detectors, the hiring of police officers, and greater use of school searches and automatic locking doors. Outside of schools, the mentality has led to the exploding security service industry, the development of gated communities, the rise of suburban sprawl, and in some cases, the making of a more unjust police force.

Concerns about violence in schools have been particularly heated during three points in the history of the United States, and each period reflects how the problem has been embroiled in broader demographic and socioeconomic realities involving immigration, prejudice, poverty, and urban and youth violence. These worries about school violence began with the building of some of the first large urban public schools in the late 19th century, waned in the early 20th century as international wars gained attention, and revived in the 1960s and early 1970s. In recent years, concerns about violence have expanded as greater availability of more deadly weapons has led to shootings in suburban schools and in urban areas. Any discussion about school violence must not neglect to account for these demographic, cultural, and economic shifts, and the ways that these realities have directed attention, shaped policy, and come together in literal and figurative ways to tell us how to go about solving the problem.

VIOLENCE IN THE CONTEXT OF HISTORY, CULTURE, AND ECONOMICS

In the late 19th century, poor immigrants from European and Asian countries were determined by some politicians and school reformers to be wild, prone to violence, and antisocial, and the common school was charged with the duty of pacifying these new arrivals. In 1846, under the leadership of Horace Mann, a Massachusetts Senate committee declared that while a poorly educated child would turn to delinquency, one "placed under the care of judicious men, taught to labor . . . be furnished with a good moral and intellectual education . . . would in nine cases out of ten, perhaps, become a good and useful citizen"; and in an 1881 report by the National Education Association, high schools were called "the most potential agency . . . to root up vice [and] to lessen crime" (both quotes from Anderson, 1998, p. 317).

While understandings about violence were often racist and classist, there was validity to the claim that cities of the 19th century were violent and that, due to their circumstances, ethnic minorities tended to be those most embroiled in the mayhem. In the 1850s and 1860s, between 40 and 80% of homicide victims and their killers were foreign-born, mainly young Irish and Germans; in Philadelphia, immigrants from Ireland, comprising about 20% of the city's population, accounted for about 30% of those indicted for homicide between 1839 and 1900; later, Italians became overrepresented in violent crime statistics (Short, 1997, p. 6).

At the time, two groups of individuals moved to the cities and sought education in the expanding public schools, and reformers responded in a number of ways. They developed pauper and compulsory education laws and created more direct links between schools and the criminal justice system (especially with the passage of the Juvenile Court Act in 1899, which established separate proceedings for youth and adults and gave power to the state to act *in loco parentis* to delinquent youth). One group of individuals—immigrants from countries such as Italy and Ireland—was mostly Catholic and poor and determined by middle-upper class and Protestant reformers in the United States to be dangerous: "Members of Catholic religious organizations, it was alleged, were sworn to commit the most diabolical and dastardly acts; and recent immigrants were said to carry vicious diseases" (Peterson, 1983, p. 227).

In a similar way, the second group, made up of individuals from rural areas who were mostly poor farmers seeking work in the factories, was considered in need of a civilizing process that could be afforded only by schools. Partly from fear and partly from compassion, 31 states enacted some form of compulsory education law by 1900 (Perkinson, 1995). These laws were, in part, a response to wayward youth—a way of getting kids off the street and into the state institution that would teach them the social mores of a conservative, Protestant, U.S. society. In schools, worries about violence were dealt with in sometimes severe ways, especially in some of the Lancasterian schools, where students were caned, paddled, and so times put in wooden shackles (Fishman, 1979).

After a short hiatus, violence in schools regained attention in the 1960s and early 1970s. This was a time when students protested against injustices throughout the United States and brought home to individuals the reality of social inequities as well as assassinations, youth protests, and rioting—all of which increased worries about violence and social upheaval. This time, the federal government intervened and forced (to some extent) desegregation and more funding for schools in the form of compensatory education and antipoverty programs. In 1977, the $2.4 million *Safe School Study*, supported by the U.S. Congress, determined that school violence was a justifiable concern. The study reported that approximately 282,000 students and 5,200 teachers were physically assaulted in secondary schools every month (National Institute of Education [NIE], 1977). It also recognized factors that until then had not been examined in great detail, reporting that crime in school neighborhoods, large classes, lax school administration, and discriminatory discipline policies also contributed to school violence.

Notions about school violence have always been developed alongside socioeconomic realities, but in the 1960s, these realities included as well the rhetoric and actions of liberation movements and critical pedagogy, and a renewed call for social consciousness—reiterated federally in the Civil Rights Act of 1964 and the Elementary and Secondary Education Act of 1965 (see Carmichael, 1997; Vinovskis, 1996). School violence was perceived by some Marxists and critical theorists as a legitimate protest against unjust school structures, including segregation, economic and school funding inequities that have devastated primarily African American and Hispanic areas, inadequate resources in schools, and curricula devoid of multicultural content.

In addition, a number of books presented a U.S. society—an "other America," in the words of Michael Harrington (1962)—that was contorting under the weight of poverty, violence, and social chaos. These books included Richard Cloward and Lloyd Ohlin's *Delinquency and Opportunity* (1960), Oscar Lewis's *The Children of Sanchez* (1961), Frank Riessman's *The Culturally Deprived Child* (1962), Michael Harrington's *The Other America* (1962), and Daniel Patrick Moynihan's report on poverty and race, *The Negro Family* (1965). Some of this literature, especially the Moynihan report, while nodding to the dire consequences of racism and poverty, tended to put focus on the deficiencies of African Americans and their inability to disrupt the cycle of poverty and violence that they were embroiled in. In some ways, though, this literature and the public policy

a response to reactionary views of delinquency and
espoused by Banfield (1958), who explained that
naturally impulsive, hostile, aggressive, and lacking

0s and 1970s, poverty and violence became in a
of the same coin. Because the ecological view recognized
ence as an outcome of poverty, a number of federal and state interventions were installed in cities to combat poverty, including Mobilization for Youth in New York, the Los Angeles Youth Project, the Chicago Area Projects, and Youth for Service in San Francisco (Decker & Van Winkle, 1996). Mobilization for Youth influenced the formulation of the War on Poverty through the President's Committee on Juvenile Delinquency (Katz, 1989, p. 80). During the Johnson administration, this committee became the focal point where concerns about poverty and violence met. It put attention on community mobilization of young people and eradication of blocked economic opportunities through job development and vocational education.

During the same period, the Commission on Law Enforcement and Administration of Justice echoed some 19th-century school reformers when it stated that the school, "unlike the family, is a public instrument for training young people. . . . It is the principle public institution for development of basic commitment by young people to the goals and values of our society" (quoted in Anderson, 1998, p. 318). The commission made a number of recommendations, which the Supreme Court in later years endorsed. It suggested, for example, that the juvenile court evolve into a two-track system with separate criminal and social-welfare functions. Public officials would divert and handle informally most minor delinquents and status offenders through alternative programs, schooling, and social interventions rather than through criminal justice processes (Feld, 1999).

Alternative schools, social interventionist programs, and a "transformed" juvenile justice system were developed to deal with delinquency by breaking what was considered a cycle of antisocial behavior that reproduced itself through strained and dysfunctional family arrangements in primarily black urban areas. This interpretation of violence as the outcome of behavior by poor and minority youth can be seen from different perspectives. To some extent, it reflects a reality supported by crime rates. As Tonry (1995) noted, African American youth are overrepresented in violent crime statistics. And as noted earlier, in the 19th century, Italians, Irish, and other ethnic minorities were most caught up in crime. But rather than just seeing their violence, we must understand how poor and minority youth have been urban casualties as well. As Tonry also noted, young black men are four times more likely than young white men to be at the receiving end of a violent act.

Embedded in the concerns of the day, government and school policies, and everyday assumptions about youth, understandings about violence have always been steered by demographics, popular movements, conceptions of poverty and race, and popular social science theories of deviance and discipline. Through the 1980s and into the 1990s violence prevention started to reflect a more punitive and legislative approach to the problem of violence: We saw the transferral of youth to adult courts and prisons; the development of "boot camps" and alternative schools run in military fashion to instill respect and obedience in the young; some degree of gun control legislation; community policing tactics; and the influx of funds for schools to develop violence prevention programs.

In addition, our understandings about violence have been shaped by issues associated with sexual harassment and violence involving girls, popularized in *Hostile Hallways* (American Association of University Women Educational Foundation & Louis Harris Associates, 1993) and given legal legitimacy in the unlikely 1999 decision by the Supreme Court to hold school districts accountable for neglecting to intervene in incidents of prolonged sexual harassment in schools. Another factor affecting the nation's reaction to school violence is rapid innovation in media, advertising, telecommunications, and computer technology. Since the 1960s, when the effects of media on violent behavior began to be scrutinized by behaviorists and psychologists, the concern about media violence has grown to a feverish pitch, with parents, researchers, and watchdog groups paying particular attention to newer "first-person shooter" video and computer games.

The school shootings in the late 1990s shifted focus away from large, predominately black ghettos to smaller cities and suburban (and even rural) areas. In interviews and conversations, in newspaper articles and television commentary, politicians, pundits, educators, and parents have bemoaned the downfall of our once safe suburbs and rural areas. They have wondered out loud about the insanity that seems to have gripped young white boys. School violence has become of significant concern at a moment of growing dissatisfaction with public schools, and at a time when reforms regarding charter schools, vouchers, and alternative and magnet schools are being considered seriously by reformers and politicians as a means of transforming and even replacing public schooling. It is a time when violence is used by some commentators and private-interest groups as a rallying cry against the apparent permissiveness that adults have shown toward young people, the perceived failure of liberal ideologies in the face of out-of-control young people, and the breakdown of families blamed at various times on divorce, poverty, and feminism. The public production of violence is seen in all these social phenomena—in our popular culture, in rhetoric that uses violence to denigrate schools, and in assumptions about young people that see them as the focus of the blame. The response to violence, then, takes place amid this clamor of history, culture, and economics.

THE POLICY PICTURE

From the 1960s into the 1980s, concern about violence in school was strong: Gallup polls voiced the anxiety of the general public, the *Safe School Study* (NIE, 1977) represented Congress-backed, large-scale studies that had begun in the 1970s, and the Drug-Free Schools and Communities Act of 1986 (PL 99-570, 1986) was but one example of legislation that followed in the path of these general concerns and federal studies. In spite of this activity, worries grew even greater and federal activity busier in the 1990s. To start the decade, the Crime Control Act of 1990 was passed by the U.S. Congress and included the Gun-Free School Zones Act (PL 101-647, 1990), which made it unlawful to carry a gun within 1,000 feet of school property or municipal playgrounds. Though the statute had been determined unconstitutional in the 1994 Supreme Court case *United States v. Lopez*, the legislation—combined with growing concern about crime and news stories depicting more tragic forms of school violence—ushered in a time of increased federal policy and funding for schools such as Brandon High.

Perhaps most influential, though, was an initiative that dealt only peripherally with school violence. This was George Bush's *America 2000* (National Governors' Association and President's Education Summit, 1991), which included as one of its six goals that "every school in America will be free of drugs and violence and will offer a disciplined environment conducive to learning" (p. 2). In response to *America 2000*, Congress passed the Safe and Drug-Free Schools and Communities Act of 1994 (PL 103-382, 1994), which in 1995 provided $630 million to states, stipulating that "drug and violence prevention programs are essential components of a comprehensive strategy to promote school safety and to reduce the demand for and use of drugs throughout the Nation" (p. 3673).

The Drug-Free Schools and Communities Act (PL 103-382, 1994) made available funding for training, professional development, technical assistance, and programs responding to violence in schools and communities (see also Hearing on School Violence, 1994). Also in 1994, Goals 2000: Educate America Act (PL 103-227), which President Clinton developed to reflect George Bush's *America 2000*, was passed. It included Title VII (Safe

Schools Act) and Title VIII (Gun-Free Schools Act). The two acts (also part of PL 103-227), taken together, represented the two faces of federal response to violence in schools: increased funding for violence-prevention programs and stiffer punishment of youth offenders.

The Safe Schools Act (PL 103-227, Sec. 701) made available grants for up to $3,000,000 for schools and other organizations throughout the United States to develop violence-prevention programs that would lead to collaborations between community-based organizations and that would seek a high level of participation by youth. These organizations needed to demonstrate, according to the policy, a strong local commitment

> to the formation of partnerships among the local educational agency, a community-based organization, a nonprofit organization with a demonstrated commitment to or expertise in developing education programs or providing educational services to students or the public, a local law enforcement agency, or any combination thereof; and a high level of youth participation in such projects or activities. (p. 205)

As a result of the Safe Schools Act, schools such as Brandon High have increased their numbers of programs aimed at addressing violence and have done so in collaboration with nonprofit groups, colleges and universities, and local police departments. Within the act's first year, by May 1995, 19 school districts in the United States had been awarded approximately $18 million in violence-prevention grants, with Chicago public schools receiving the largest sum—$3 million.

In general, the money was spent on conflict-resolution and peer mediation programs, counseling for crime victims, training for school personnel, parent involvement in prevention efforts, and planning for comprehensive, long-term violence-prevention strategies. Since the focus of the Safe Schools Act was on partnerships and violence-prevention programs (and not security), only 5% of a grant could be used for metal detectors and security personnel. However, in 1998, Representative Martin Frost (D-Texas) introduced a bill through the Safe Schools Act that would establish a $175 million initiative to help schools hire police officers.

The Gun-Free Schools Act (PL 103-227, Sec. 1031), on the other hand, addressed violence with a focus on punishment and by drawing more definitive connections between schools and the criminal justice system. It required the expulsion of a student for not less than 1 year if it has been determined that a student brought a gun to school, and, as Noguera (1995) noted, ushered in various forms of zero-tolerance policies to schools. Passed by Congress in 1994 along with the Safe Schools Act, and largely a result of President Clinton's Goals 2000: Educate America Act, the Gun-Free Schools Act states that

> no assistance may be provided to any local educational agency under this Act unless such agency has in effect a policy requiring the expulsion from school for a period of not less than one year of any student who is determined to have brought a weapon to a school under the jurisdiction of the agency except such policy may allow the chief administering officer of the agency to modify such expulsion requirement for a student on a case-by-case basis. (p. 270)

While it made room for expulsion policies to be modified on a case-by-case basis, the Gun-Free Schools Act has had the effect of enforcing a rigid and sometimes unjust form of discipline in schools. The reality of zero tolerance goes beyond weapons. For example, in 1997, Senator Jesse Helmes introduced an amendment to the Gun-Free Schools Act that would require local educational agencies to expel not only students who brought weapons to school, but also students in possession of an illegal drug or drug paraphernalia.

By the end of 1995, 47 states had enacted laws or policies that called for zero tolerance. While the Gun-Free Schools Act did not make available funds in the way the Safe Schools Act did, as an amendment to the Elementary and Secondary Education Act of 1965 it required that federal funding be withheld from a school that did not comply with the requirements set forth by the act. The law had to be implemented in a fashion consistent with the Individuals with Disabilities Education Act (IDEA) and Section 504 of the Rehabilitation Act of 1973, which mandated that a student with a disability be expelled only if it is determined that bringing a firearm to school was not a manifestation of the student's disability and after procedural safeguards were followed. The 1997 reauthorization of IDEA stated that disabled students could not be suspended for more than 10 days unless they brought a gun to school, in which case they may be suspended for up to 45 days.

As a result of this act, schools such as Brandon High have revised their disciplinary policies. Their newer approaches to discipline have come down hardest on poor and nonwhite students, who are most often on the receiving end of punishment. As Fuentes (1998, p. 20) noted, "Zero tolerance is the mantra in public schools and juvenile courts, and what it really means is that to be young is to be suspect" (see also Block, 1997; Epp, 1996; Pitch, 1995). Here, public policy (as typified by the Gun-Free Schools Act) melds with popular conceptions of youth to create a general message that repeats loudly and endlessly: *Kids are out of control and adults better put the reins on and quit coddling them.*

WHERE POLICY MEETS THE SCHOOL

As a kind of distant tribe that has gone wild, according to many public conceptions, students are at varying times "hormone-driven," "out of control," "lacking morality," and "too easily influenced" (see Lesko, 1996; Miller, 1998). At Brandon High, as elsewhere, discussions with adults about teenagers inevitably led to shakes of the head and reminders of days long gone when youngsters heeded adult expectations and an educator could teach a class without feeling threatened. School staff seemed always to want the best for their students at the same time that they feared, worried about, and sometimes disliked them.

But many relationships between teachers and students at Brandon High were not fraught with such tensions. At times classrooms during free periods were converted into quiet hangouts for students, sanctuaries away from the crowded hallways, where students could have a reprieve from worries or avoid particular students with whom they did not get along. In these classrooms, students sat on desks or lounged on heating vents and talked with a caring teacher who seemed to enjoy the company. While no angels, these students were not likely to have serious problems in school. They participated in school activities, got along with most teachers, and generally would not be suspended or expelled for violent actions (see Warner, Weist, & Krulak, 1999, p. 60).

And yet, some of these academically and socially successful students also went through their school days in ways that could be violent: Even some of the best students were at times bullies, individuals who harassed girls, who made threats or demonstrated prejudices. As in most schools, vicious language and harassment were aimed at gay, nonwhite, and poor students; girls; disabled students; and students of nonstandard body size and looks, and were as likely to come from "good" kids as those deemed "bad." Though largely ignored by social policy, these too are forms of violence that are committed by a range of students and can escalate into more overt kinds of attacks.

Consider a single incident that I saw at Brandon High. A white student takes down a thumbtack from a bulletin board near the main office and gently sticks the buttocks of a black girl who is passing by. The boy and girl know each other. The girl is surprised, looks angry but does not protest, and tells the boy (whom she knows by name) that she will get him back. All of this takes about 5 seconds, then both leave in separate directions and go to their classes.

The time needed to unravel this episode is more than most school staff have, and the questions that must be asked go beyond what most policy can deal with. Was this action a form of sexual harassment? Was it racially motivated? Does a thumbtack constitute a weapon, so will the boy be ex-pelled? Was this an example of naughty but natural frolicking between the sexes? What if the two are friends? Was the boy the criminal and the girl the victim—and will they remain so if the girl does in fact get the boy back, perhaps with a longer thumbtack?

Policy paints a pretty neat picture of violence: a problem involving weapons that can be cured by prevention programs, such as Drug Abuse Resistance Education (DARE) and peer mediation, and "get-tough" mea-sures associated with police officers and zero tolerance. But violence at Brandon High was an ongoing problem involving not only fights and occa-sionally weapons, but also ambiguous incidents such as the one involving the thumbtack, as well as cases involving harassment, bullying, systemic violence, and even suicide. Some schools attempt to address these problems through character education, classroom talks about depression, tolerance lectures in auditoriums, and even in some sex education classes, but these forms of violence prevention are usually the reserve of elementary and mid-dle schools. In high schools, while efforts are geared toward harassment, suicide, and bullying prevention, most efforts are responses to fears associ-ated with weapon and gang violence. The more subtle realities involving girls and violence, self-mutilation and self-destructive behavior, hidden forms of taunting and death threats, and the violence that emanates from the institution itself are, while less fatal, more prevalent than the kinds of tragedies associated with gun violence, and yet are of less interest to most policymakers.

THE CITY AND THE SCHOOL

Following the arrival of Father LeMoyne, a Jesuit missionary, in what is now Brandon city, early white settlers came to the upstate New York area because they were attracted to the salt mines, limestone and salina rock quarries, and fertile farmland, which the Iroquois had appreciated for many years before them. By 1803, 60 settlers involved in salt mining moved into the swamp area and built two mills, a tavern, and several houses (O'Neill, 1988). One settler, James Geddes, was the surveyor for the Erie Canal and oversaw the building of the 363-mile waterway, a portion of which passed through Brandon city, turning this sleepy upstate area into a boom town. Between 1820 and 1830, when the canal opened, the popula-tion of Brandon city almost tripled. In 1825 the area was incorporated as a village. Then, in 1848, the legislature drew up a charter making the vil-lage a city, and appointed Alfred Salisbury its first superintendent of schools (Fowler, 1969). The first high school was built in 1855.

From the 19th century into the 20th, the city was transformed from a mining and farming hub to a factory city known for its electronic equipment, air conditioners, washing machines, office machines, chinaware, automotive gears, floodlights, and metal stampings and garment pressing machines. In more recent years, however, Brandon city has been described as "a smaller Pittsburgh" (Grant, 1988) and like Pittsburgh has undergone devastating de-industrialization and the loss of many blue-collar and professional jobs. Many of the city's major employers, including General Electric, Carrier Corp., Solvay, Crucible Steel Co., and Chrysler Corp., among others, have closed, moved elsewhere, or downsized. In 1965, the population of Brandon city was about 219,000 and officials projected that the city's population would rise to 222,000 by 1980, but by 1990, the population had dropped to about 163,000 inhabitants (City Chamber of Commerce, 1965; U.S. Bureau of the Census, 1990). Though Irish, Germans, and Italians still made up about 40% of the city's population in 1990, many of the middle-to-upper-class Italians, Irish, Germans, Jews, and other Euro-Americans left the city for the expanding suburbs, and the African American population more than doubled primarily because of migration from the south of the United States. Student enrollment from the 1960s to the 1990s dropped from about 30,000 students to just over 23,000. In 1990, the median household income was about $21,000 with over 22% of the people living in poverty.

Brandon High School is located on the south side of Brandon city, not far from a major highway that splits the city in half, in an area that is primarily poor and African American but abuts a rather wealthy community that is primarily white. Brandon High was built in 1965 and is one of four high schools in the city. There are about 1,400 students in the school, about half of them African American, half Caucasian. There is a small minority of Latino and Native American students as well. About 41% of the students are eligible for the free breakfast program. At the time of my research, the school had one principal, four assistant principals, five counselors, a psychologist, a social worker, a police officer and security guards, dropout-prevention staff, and about 90 teachers. Since the early 1990s, the school has had programs and committees aimed at reducing violence, including the Peer Mediation Program, the Crisis Intervention Team, the Student Support Team, and a DARE program. The school is considered one of the better public schools in the city, though during the 1997–1998 school year there was an article in the city's primary newspaper targeting Brandon High as a particularly violent school.

I have seen in Brandon High what Anderson (1999) referred to as a "code of the street"—a set of informal rules that govern the public behavior of young people in urban areas. In his research, Anderson described parents in Philadelphia whose lives were fraught with daily struggles to protect their children. He described youth who must adapt to a presentation that is threatening, and accept in themselves a willingness to turn violent in order to garner respect and to protect themselves. Here, middle-class black youth must learn to code-switch by having aspirations for bright futures and by avoiding criminality at the same time that they maneuver themselves through streets where middle-class and poor black families live together and a code of violence rules.

On the south side of Brandon city, as well, I found gang posturing and aggression that went hand in hand with a code of conduct steeped in violence. Some young people were so thoroughly a part of this code that a suggestion by school staff that they not act violently led to smirks, shakes of the head—indications that adults just did not understand. We cannot write off the real violence that some kids do, but neither can we forget our own informal rules and codes that have paved the way for our national and school-based responses to violence—which have, in some cases, created more problems for youth. In Brandon High, and other schools, what Anderson (1999) explained as a deeply environmental problem endemic to the circumstances of neighborhoods is too often dealt with in a slate-clearing manner that penalizes youth for the circumstances that adults too have helped to create.

ENTERING BRANDON HIGH

Beside the driveway that leads to the high school, there is a sign with removable letters that says "Welcome to Brandon High" and lists the weekly events occurring at the school—a basketball game, the senior prom, a meeting with parents, a yearbook club meeting. The sign is well tended; the grass around its posts is kept trim and graffiti are quickly removed. Below the sign, winding down to the school, is a road that circles around the front of the building and into the parking lot. In the center of the circle is a large patch of grass where evacuated students stand during fire drills and bomb threats. One area of the parking lot is reserved for student parking, another for teacher parking. Often a police car is parked in the teacher parking area, clashing with the rest of the cars because of its blue and white colors, and its "DARE Kids To Resist Drugs and Violence" and "School's Out, Drive Carefully" bumper stickers.

A sidewalk follows the circle to the parking lot, and along the sidewalk is a cement wall about 4 feet high where students sit—some smoking cigarettes, some listening to Walkmans, and some talking—during their study halls and lunch periods. The same faces appear outside each day. At one end of the wall, closest to the school, students—most of them white—in baggy pants, flannel button-down shirts, baseball caps, and overcoats meet with friends, sometimes bouncing in place to keep warm against the winter cold. The girls wear platform shoes, with soles that can be 6 inches high, ultra-wide bellbottoms and oversized T-shirts, and coats that hang close to their knees—a kind of hippie, hobo, hip-hopper look. At the other end of the wall, mostly African American students come together. The boys wear low-hanging jeans and khakis—a style sometimes attributed to prison culture where inmates are not permitted to wear belts—with Boxer Joe labels peeking out the back, New York Yankee ski hats covering close-cropped hair, and red, white, and blue Tommy Hilfiger shirts. The girls wear dark-colored dresses and skirts and high-heeled shoes, and carry large handbags. Some are outfitted in hip-hopper clothes, which for many school staff represent the new presence of serious girl gangs. The girls usually stand along the wall passing Walkmans to each other, sometimes standing away from the boys, sometimes using their handbags to protect their hot-ironed and gel-straightened hair from the persistently drizzly cold weather of Brandon city.

Beyond the sidewalk is the school: a three-story brick building that carries scars where graffiti have been sandblasted off the brick facade. "Brandon High School" is over the doors of the school. At one point during the year the *d* was missing, was replaced, fell off again, and remained off. The entrance to the school is eight doors wide—four sets of double doors. In the mornings, as students come in, only one door is unlocked, which is part of the school's "single-point entry" policy. Each student must pass before the entrance monitor. Throughout the day, the monitor remains at the main entrance, at times taking a break from the tedium by drinking coffee or reading the newspaper at her desk. All visitors must sign a book at her desk, specifying "name," "destination," "time in," and "time out." With her Brandon city newspaper at the ready, the monitor is always willing to talk about the daily news as visitors come into the school. The wide entranceway of the school, where her desk is located, is bordered by two hallways and the cafeteria. Through the large glass windows of the cafeteria, one can see the long Formica cafeteria tables and plastic chairs set up in rows.

Given the central location of the cafeteria, the smell of mass-produced food fills the first floor of the school. Around here, Detective O'Hara, the school police officer, is usually found, keeping an eye on what is going on in the cafeteria, in the main entranceway, and down the two main corridors. The walls are cinderblock, painted a muted pink. Lines of ink are scratched into some walls where students drag their pens as they walk to classes. When lunch is in session, the cafeteria is crowded with students socializing, eating, making plans for the evening, finishing or copying some homework—all within the half hour that is allotted for lunch. When lunch period is not in session, individuals or small groups of students can be seen sitting at the ends of the long tables, sometimes chatting, sometimes with notebooks and textbooks spread before them. At times, larger groups of students—the Honor Society or the Yearbook Club—meet to discuss upcoming events while cafeteria workers, all of them African American, clean the tables and mop the floor.

Down the corridors off the main entrance, a trophy case heralds the athletic successes of the school, a billboard outlines the contributions of "Famous African American Scientists," another glass case advertises the peer mediation program with a T-shirt that reads "When Peers Meet, People Listen," and offices and classrooms interrupt the endless columns of gray metal lockers. The smell of lunchroom food seems to come out of the lockers themselves, the call of students from one end of the hall to another is ongoing, and walkie-talkies squawk continually. Between classes, students meet around their lockers to gather books and talk. There will be quiet for a moment, then the crashing of locker doors being slammed shut as students are urged along by hall monitors to get to class. The school police officer is always walking the halls. He seems to be everywhere at once. He talks to students in quiet tones, telling them to "get out of your lockers and get into your classrooms." There is the crash-slam of lockers again. Students move to their classes along the right sides of the hallways, following the same rules as do drivers. To be walking along the left side of the hallway inevitably means a block or a push from oncoming crowds. Students shove each other, play-fight; a boy will snap the bra of a girl, or swat another boy with old textbooks. Students inadvertently mop the floors with the dragging cuffs of their oversized pants; some boys bounce imaginary basketballs and take layup shots against the lockers; an occasional wad of paper sails into the air and becomes lost in the crowd.

Just before classes are about to begin, teachers stand outside their classrooms beckoning students to get in. Pairs of lovers wait until the very last moment to obey. When the bell blares, these lingering couples slowly kiss before departing. Groups of boys give each other handshakes—"pops," or knocking their knuckles together—before splitting up. As the hallways clear, Janice Street, the principal, comes out of her office and checks the corridors to make sure students are doing what they are supposed to do. She clears the last-minute hall wanderers with a threat of suspension. These students move out of her sight, only sometimes going to class. Back in the office, the principal continues with her work. When not in the hall, she seems forever attached to a phone and stacks of paper. Behind the main office's large counter, women are busy at work, answering phones, preparing the daily announcements, speaking into walkie-talkies. Substitute teachers are often found standing along the high counter that separates the small waiting area from the office. Students, looking solemn, are seated in the waiting area working on excuses—why they missed class, why they had a Walkman in school, why they wrote on the bathroom wall—before meeting with the principal. Other students are usually milling around waiting to get the attention of an office worker in order to use a phone, to retrieve something a family member had dropped off, or to ask about an upcoming test or event.

Off the main office, down a short hallway, is the guidance area—a suite with four offices and a meeting room—boasting a large computer-generated sign that reads "Counseling and Guidance Department." In this area, the atmosphere is more calm than in the hallways and main office. There are banners on the walls advertising colleges: Siena, Cornell, Niagara, Geneseo, Oswego, Rensselaer, Hobart, among others, with assorted picturesque posters of sun-filled college campuses. On the counter are pamphlets for the Army, Marines, and Air Force. Taped to the wall is an article entitled "Where the Jobs Will Be," notices about the SAT and ACT tests, and a financial aid chart. There is also a poster on the wall for Teenline, a teenage emergency hotline, and for Booth House, a home for runaway teens. The secretary's desk is located in the center of the suite, surrounded by gray file cabinets. She too seems always attached to a phone and paperwork. She speaks to parents, organizes students' records, and schedules screening committee meetings for students who wish to be readmitted to school after being suspended or expelled.

Between the main office and the guidance suite is Detective O'Hara's office, though he is more often in the hallways than in his office. His door is always open, but he keeps his handcuffs and pepper spray locked in his desk drawer. On his wall are posters that warn students of the detrimental effects of drugs, alcohol, and violence, and public service messages listing phone numbers to use and places to go to report violence and to seek city and police help. His police academy diploma hangs prominently behind his desk next to a tall file cabinet. Taped to the door of his office is a newspaper article reporting on the Officer Friendly Program. This is a student-mentor initiative between the city police department and the Brandon city school district, which is part of the police department's attempts to improve relations between police and youth. The article shows a picture of Officer Esposito, the Brandon High DARE teacher, sitting with a young African American third-grader whom he mentors as part of the program. During most days, Officer Esposito, in his full police uniform, uses Detective O'Hara's office to prepare for his classes and to take advantage of the telephone to make last-minute calls to other schools or to his girlfriend.

Meanwhile, Detective O'Hara is continually in and out of his office. He will make a phone call to the police department about a student or a charge that has been filed, or continue endless paperwork, but then he is out in the hallways again, urging students to "get a set of brains" and attempting to convince people in the building that all is well and under control until he leaves at the end of the day as the last afternoon school students depart at 6:00.

BEING DOWN

When Pattillo-McCoy (1999) described the black middle-class neighborhood of Chicago that was the focus of her research, she did so by noting the diversity in the neighborhood; Groveland was a community where drug dealers rubbed elbows with university students and gang turf extended a block or two beyond empty lots and into the comfortable households of the black professionals—hospital workers, teachers, salespeople, and postal workers. It was a community where the hard-working caretakers of well-tended lawns were sometimes only one misfortune away from an economic and social down-spin; a place where clean sidewalks and thriving civic groups and churches belied the reality of poor public services, segregation, and the incessant pull on youth of the fast life.

Brandon High is in a neighborhood in some ways similar to the community that Pattillo-McCoy (1999) described. The pull of the fast life, the rubbing of elbows between the various classes of both white and black students, the variety of experiences, the feeling that the school and other institutions were good but only a short step away from decline, shape the manners of the people who live in the area and attend the schools. Here, pastel-painted ranch houses stand side-by-side with litter-strewn streets and boarded-up storefronts, and even the most socially isolated kids are in contact with middle-class and professional entities such as the school.

In many ways, Brandon High was a regular small-city school in a neighborhood that had a diverse mix of people and backgrounds. But though there was this variety and mixing, as in other schools, students seemed always attached to particular groups—what some adults like to call "peer groups" and what students referred to as their "homeys" or "home-girls," or the "fellas they're down with." In interviews, students often described themselves by saying, "I'm down with these people," or "I ain't down with them." As in the school Eckert (1989) studied, adults judged students according to the groups of which each was a part. From the perspective of most adults in the school, being a member of the "jocks" or "queens" was generally good; being down with the "burnouts," the "gang-bangers," or the "druggies" was not. These groups were real and always visible in the self-segregated cafeteria and parking lot of the school, in the racial makeup of afternoon school and tracked classes, and in the membership roles of extracurricular activities. These dynamic and deeply personal groups moved through Brandon High interacting with other groups, sometimes peacefully, sometimes not.

For me, the refrain "being down" took on new dimensions as I noticed students not only being down with particular groups of students, but also being down at the bottom of the school hierarchy or being down emotionally. My attempts to interact with the students and staff at the school were also attempts to be down with them, to share my thoughts and experiences as they shared theirs. But I was forever a foreigner in the school: not teacher, not police officer, not counselor, not student, and not administrator—but researcher, a designation that some students and teachers did not quite understand. "What do you do?" was a question that many asked and in my attempts to answer them, I described my research and my belief that it was important to work with schools to help make violence a thing of the past—regardless of how utopian that may sound.

CHAPTER 2

Violence in the Organization of Schooling

In the hallway on the third floor of Brandon High there was a sudden commotion. James Maddy, the coordinator of the afternoon school program and a special education teacher, who was on hall duty at the time, was called to the scene on his walkie-talkie. I happened to be standing with him at the time and he told me to come along in case he needed "backup." As he trotted down the hall and I followed hesitantly (not thrilled by the idea of being backup), he mumbled more to himself than to me: "Here we go again. Another fight."

The calls of students became louder as we approached. By the time we came to the corridor, two girls, one African American and one Hispanic, were on the floor tangled around each other, kicking, punching, and scratching. One girl was trying to scratch the face of the other while the other pulled the hair of the first in steady, hard yanks. Amid the shouts and the commotion, two teachers attempted to keep onlooking students in classrooms, but some of the students were cheering the two fighters on. Another teacher was struggling to hold a leg of each of the fighting girls high in the air so that they would not be able to stand up. The girls were swearing back and forth repeatedly, calling each other "fuckin' whores." The black girl yelled that she was going to kill the Hispanic girl.

James Maddy had the two girls nearly separated and calm when the African American girl broke free, ran between us, and began kicking the other girl as hard as she could. The other girl was still on the floor holding her hand to a deep fingernail scratch on her face. The Hispanic girl yelled and kicked back and the teacher pushed the two girls apart, slapping the Hispanic girl's face. The Hispanic girl yelled at the teacher, "I'll kick your white ass!" The teacher yelled back, "Shut up! Shut up!" Things were quite out of control.

The teacher held one girl's leg up in the air again. James Maddy had the other girl calm now and was escorting her to the main office. As she passed she was primarily ignored by white students, but other African American students—mostly girls—asked her what had happened. Some chastised her for fighting, saying, "Now you're out of here," meaning suspended from school. The girl kept telling the other students, "I kicked that fat-ass cheerleader's ass!" Two students cheered her for doing so; another told her it was a stupid thing to do.

The girls were separated: One was sent to the main office, the other to the guidance suite. In the guidance suite, James Maddy told the Hispanic girl to wait: "Just don't move!" She stood next to the secretary's desk breathing heavily, tense, still pumped from the fight. The secretary moved away from her. Students waiting to see their counselors watched her. One asked, "What you here for?" and the girl told her, "I got into a fight." Another student wanted to know whom she was fighting, and the girl told him, "Some cheerleader." This seemed to suffice: In a school where group affiliation can trump individuality, "Cheerleader" was as good as a name. Finally, an assistant principal found an empty office and told the girl to go in and wait. The girl sat in the office in a plastic chair looking out the window. Brian Arena, another assistant principal, came in, dropped some papers on the chair next to the girl, and told her that she was suspended for 5 days and that she needed to schedule a judicial hearing at the Board of Education Building. Starting in November 1997, as a result of the city's new zero-tolerance policy, all students caught fighting in school were summoned to a formal judicial hearing.

Mr. Arena stood by a file cabinet, looking at the student while the student looked out the window. He lectured her for fighting again, saying, "When are you going to learn? This is your second time." He told her "that's strike two." Last year the same two girls had gotten into a fight, though last year's fight, according to Mr. Arena, was less brutal. Mr. Arena gave the student a form to sign. It specified why she was suspended ("fighting") and that, according to district policy, she must report to the Family Center for the 5 days of her suspension to be tutored for 2 hours each day. The girl said that she could not go. If she was suspended, and social services found out, she would lose her child care support. The assistant principal told her to bring her son. "After all, it's a family center," he said, either ignoring or missing the point. The form that he gave the student said that students would not lose any class time or fall behind in their schoolwork while suspended at the Family Center, though of course they did. Several students who had been in fights and had gone to the Family Center remarked that they fell far behind in their work and that sometimes their tutors did not show up for their instruction.

SYSTEMIC VIOLENCE

In spite of its intensity—the brutality, the vicious language, the swift disciplinary procedures, the striking of the student by the teacher—the hallway fight was not unusual at Brandon High, or at other high schools. In Brandon's cafeteria, it was not uncommon to hear the shout of "Fight!" followed by the sudden turning of chairs, the opening of doors, and the movement of students rushing either away from or toward the fight. One student spoke for many when she noted, "If you sit in enough lunches you're bound to see a fight." At Brandon High, 53 students were suspended for fighting during the first 4 months of the 1997–1998 school year. Of the 53 students, 31 were girls, 22 boys. All but 8 were African American. In total, between September 1, 1997, and January 8, 1998, there were 584 suspensions given (sometimes in-school suspension) for a range of offenses, some minor, some not.

While the numbers no doubt fluctuate, in other city high schools the number of black and Latino students suspended for fighting (and other offenses) is significantly higher than that of white students. While it is true that it appears that most fights are between nonwhite students, in general suspension is meted out more rapidly to poorer and African American students than to others (Report by the Advancement Project and The Civil Rights Project, 2000; Soriano, Soriano, & Jimenez, 1994). McQuillan (1998, p. 85) observed that "differential application of school discipline according to students' perceived social status is commonplace," and Davidson (1996, p. 123) reported that nonwhite students were "disproportionately subject to disciplinary action" and often lacked the family support to challenge unjust suspensions and expulsions.

Also typical of this fight was that it was between girls. For Brandon High staff, and staff at other schools, there was concern and even shock regarding the number of girls who fought. The school principal, two guidance counselors, the school police officer, and several teachers and students expressed their concern about what was typically referred to as "girl fighting." While part of this concern reflects stereotypes that indicate that girls should not fight and therefore their fights are viewed more critically and noticed more readily than those involving boys, it is probable that girls are fighting physically and more brutally now than ever before (Artz, 1998; Sikes, 1997; Stein, 1995). During one week at Brandon High, there were five fights, all between girls. One student described the chaos that accompanies altercations, but also referred naturally to girls when describing a fight:

> It's just like all of a sudden you hear somebody yell "Fight!" and like everybody rushes around to see. People are really serious, like girls

are pulling out the other girls' weaves and people are just—they don't even care about what's around them. This one time, this fight between two girls broke out right in front of me on the second floor. And everybody just bomb rushed it. And I was like, just let me out! Let me out! And it's not like they are going to just let you out. I mean they're not going to let you out of it unless I really push myself out. It's just like crazy. And like people get injured. People are cheering and stuff. I mean it's like, for some people it's fun watching two people beating each other up.

Due in part to the swift disciplinary responses to fights by school staff, the causes of such fights are rarely discussed. In interviews and discussions, female students would sometimes discuss circumstances in ways that took into account their home lives, respect, clothes, and being "picked on." In response, the school could give one of a host of punishments.

At Brandon High, while most students were suspended for about 3 days, some were given 5 days' suspension. Some students were deemed "behavioral problems" and they were sent to the city's Alternative School. Students who were caught with a weapon would be sent to TAIP school (TAIP is an acronym for The Answer Is Peace). The school—considered by most to be a type of alternative school—was the result of the ever-expanding system of "outplacements" that developed in the school district as fears of violence increased. At the time of my research, it was located in a poor section of the city, a gang area dubbed by the local news station "the most dangerous corner in the city."

Students who were deemed unfit for any type of public institution—even TAIP—would be placed on Homebound Instruction. Homebound could last for up to a year. While on Homebound, students were required to receive instruction from a tutor who visited the house or met the student at a nearby public library. Essentially, these students were kicked out of school. They were not even allowed to take part in the afternoon school program, TAIP, or the Alternative School.

Strict and exclusionary discipline policy at Brandon High was much influenced by a November 6, 1997, letter from the superintendent of the city school district to all parents with school-age children. The letter introduced a new zero-tolerance policy that was meant to combat school fighting. The letter read, in part:

Dear Parents,
    With the increase of reported gang violence in our city, we want to assure you the [city] School District will take all necessary precautions to prevent the violence from entering our schools. Lately, how-

ever, the number of student fights in the high schools has been escalating, resulting in a disruption of the learning process. We have tried talking to students, warning them, placing them in the In-School Suspension Program, and suspending them for up to three days out of school. Nothing seems to affect those few disruptive, aggressive, violent students.

To address this threat to student safety, as of October 30, 1997, I have instituted the following: High school students involved in fights or committing assaults on students or staff members will be suspended from school and subject to a Superintendent's Hearing. If found guilty, the students may be transferred to another school or placed in one of our alternative high school programs. This placement means a change of school and, most likely, will result in a change of courses, teachers, hours of school, and inability to participate in interscholastic sports. If the student has a record of aggressive violent acts, there is a very good chance the student will not be allowed to attend any regular program and will be placed on homebound instruction.

For school staff who are fearful and guided by punishment-driven and judicial methods of retaliation against aggressive and troubled students, such disciplinary actions may seem like necessary responses to violence. But for students caught fighting in the hallway, and for others whose actions are wrong but not necessarily *criminal*, the punishment too is a form of violence. As Freire (1970), Foucault (1980), and Bourdieu (1991) noted, and as I argue throughout this book, violence can be systemic in nature. It can generate from a system of policies and practices that cancels out the life chances of students who need help, direction, and care.

Systemic violence refers to institutional forms of restriction, oppression, and brutality that can be state and nationally mandated and that trigger enforcement of rules and actions that demean, hurt, or sometimes kill people less powerful and influential than those committing the violence (Watkinson, 1996). The ramifications of the superintendent's letter, combined with a crackdown on kids in general, clears the way for drastic and sometimes unjust disciplinary policies (Block, 1997; Noguera, 1995). Essentially, individual students at Brandon High were no longer thought of as unique cases. As noted earlier, their fights were not examined and assessed. Rather, the zero-tolerance policy made way for a kind of slate-clearing approach to fights: hallways, cafeterias, and classrooms were promptly cleared of disruptive students through suspension, expulsion, and the use of alternative placements. Students might be escorted out of the school, or be kept within the building.

After being suspended for fighting or disruptive behavior (and sometimes truancy), some students would be placed in the afternoon school program, which operated from 3:00 to 6:00 each day in the basement of the school. During these hours, the school could seem lonely and empty. Like other outplacements, afternoon school was the result of policies that supported the removal of "problem students" from day school. But these students were not so much "out" as on their way out. In May 1998 there were 105 students in the afternoon school program, but about 400 students enter and exit the program throughout the year, most either dropping out or receiving a GED diploma.

While the administration insisted that their afternoon school program helped students who could not attend day school (because of a job or a child)—which was true at times—and helped students who were interested only in a GED diploma or were apparently more interested in manual labor than academics, it was also a form of tracking. In afternoon school, groups of students either worked individually on GED packets or completed "seat work." In addition, students played cards, hung out in the hallways, sneaked away to smoke outside, and in one class watched Star Trek movies with the teacher. Many students felt trapped in the afternoon school program at Brandon High. And given that attendance in this and other programs is not strictly enforced, it becomes for some students a jumping-off point for dropping out of school (see also Fine, 1991). Most students in the afternoon school had very poor attendance, even those who had chosen to be there, and they were rarely reprimanded for not coming. Some students had as many as 60 absences. Failure to urge these students to come to school sent the message that their attendance did not matter. When students knew that the school felt this way about them, many did not come.

One girl who ended up in afternoon school before dropping out expressed her situation in a way that reflected the stories of other students who violated school fighting and weapon policies and were treated in ways that were unfair. Latoya was an African American student, extremely quiet, who had transferred to Brandon High after failing out of a private Catholic school (she had failed theology several times). Her father, who was very religious, had been addicted to drugs and had gone to rehabilitation. As with other students who acted violently, there had been incidents of domestic violence in her home. Soon after the superintendent's letter was distributed and reported in the main city newspaper, Latoya was suspended and then put in the afternoon school program for bringing a knife into a school dance. She explained:

> I kind of regret getting kicked out because I miss it. This year hasn't
> been a good year. I got into a little trouble in the beginning of the

year. It wasn't my fault. It was my fault but it wasn't intentional. It was the first dance here, it started at dark time and I live in a very bad neighborhood [near TAIP school]. And me not knowing that they would have checked my pockets and bag. I wasn't intentionally coming, "Oh I'm going to fight someone at the dance." It was just my protection because I have to walk and it was nighttime. They had a little metal detector. I had a little pen that was the size of that [shows her pinky], it had a little blade at the tip. It was like the size of an art knife. I had it in my pocket and they asked me what was it. I pulled it out and gave it to them like I forgot I had it on me and so they let me in the dance. I thought I wasn't in trouble because I gave it to them and I wasn't going to fight nobody. When the dance was over, they came to me and said, "You know you are going to get in trouble." But they also made fun of it [the homemade knife], saying, "What are you going to do with this little thing?" [and] laughing. I was just going to class that Monday when I came to school, they called me to the office and said I was going to get suspended for five days.

For protection, Latoya brought the homemade blade to the dance. It was a type of knife other students had told me how to make: Melt one end of the plastic casing of a pen and press a razor blade into it. When the plastic is dry the pen becomes a makeshift blade. On the night of the dance, Latoya was working the night shift at the local supermarket. When she got off from work she had to walk through a neighborhood she feared—and with good reason. During my research with police officers who patrolled this area, officers made sure that I knew I should not come around the neighborhood when I was not with them, protected by their blue-and-white cruiser from the primarily African American boys who walked the streets in their Nike, Guess, and Tommy Hilfiger clothing and hooded sweatshirts.

At school on Monday, Latoya had told the principal that her father had given her the knife and her father, in court, had stood by the story, though she admitted in private that she had made the knife herself. Latoya had never been in trouble before at Brandon High, had never been suspended, had not been in a fight. In fact, almost nobody knew her. She was, in many ways, an invisible student. She insisted:

I never been in trouble, I never had a record, never been in a fight, suspended, nothing. They gonna suspend me for 5 days, they had no mercy or nothing. That's what really made me think of the difference between Bishop Serrano [the private school she attended] and Brandon, because Bishop Serrano you can do a lot of stuff in there and they had the heart to forgive, even if you never been in trouble, they talk to you, you know. She [the principal at Brandon] was like, well you're suspended, wrote the paper, there's nothing you can say about that. They put me in this program that started at 11:00 to 1:00 at the Family Center. I had to walk over there for a whole week. I really didn't have any work because the teacher didn't have me do nothing. They tried to put me in the afternoon school . . . I mean, for a little knife for protection for walking up here. They was gonna try and put me in afternoon school. [The principal] recommended that I went to afternoon school until November 1st. That really upset me. Because me being a senior, I had goals and everything. That side-tracked me big time. They didn't give me a chance.

Latoya was back in regular school when I spoke to her. During the school year, her attendance became more sporadic. She told me that she did not have many friends in school and was not happy. She had mentioned that she wanted to attend the local community college but when I tried to give her an application, I could not find her in school. It seemed she had left school, but the records office could not be sure since there was no paperwork about her dropping out. This kind of entrance and exit of students was not considered abnormal at Brandon High. Teachers and administrators expected that as many as 30% of their students would not receive a standard high school diploma.

Systemic violence led to unquestioned policies and actions that were at the very least demeaning and at times devastating for some students. It negatively affected not only individuals but also the environment of the school and relationships between people. Early in the school year, the administration—responding to increased fighting—instituted a policy that restricted all students to their classrooms for the day when a fight occurred at school. As a form of doublespeak, these days were called "learning" or "focus" days. This policy not only enforced a kind of prison mentality on the school, but also undermined educational opportunity for all students, who could not then go to the library, get extra help during their free periods, use the bathroom during class, or make an important phone call. Students who were academically successful and those who were failing their classes criticized the policy. Several students referred to focus days as "lockdowns." Girls, especially, complained that they needed to use bathrooms for reasons they preferred to keep to themselves.

Systemic violence made people's actions ugly in spite of the semi-innocent nature of it. Epp (1996, p. 1) wrote that "systemic violence is not intentional harm visited on the unlucky by vicious individuals. Rather, it is the unintentional consequences of procedures implemented by well-meaning authorities in a belief that the practices are in the best interests of students." The practices set in place by zero-tolerance measures are generally thought of by school staff as natural and necessary ways of dealing with students whose actions are inappropriate or violent. They are as much prevention strategies—strategies for the good of the entire school—as they are discipline policies (see also Foucault, 1975/1995, p. 109).

Yet while the presence of guards, armed police officers, surveillance cameras, metal detectors, and monitors with walkie-talkies may adequately indicate a prison, these elements should not be indicative of a school. Nobody wants to work, never mind learn, in such an environment. Nor should school faculty feel so threatened and powerless that such forms of discipline and policing appear necessary. That so many teachers and administrators are truly fearful of students and feel strong pressure to keep control of the school—to avoid the possibility of bad publicity—also gives impetus to behaviors that can be oppressive and damaging.

Such forms of violence prevention sometimes slipped into restrictions of civil rights. At times, in the name of violence prevention, students were not allowed to leave classrooms, talk to each other, or attend certain school functions. Sometimes students were also prevented from coming to school. Throughout the day at Brandon High, school staff barred the way of certain students who tried to enter. Often they were expelled or suspended students, sometimes recent graduates with friends still in school. To see so many students suspended and expelled—or "dropped from the list"—and then to see so many turned away from entering the building has to cause us to question just how public our public schools are.

Perhaps most disheartening about systemic violence is the means by which impossible scenes become everyday occurrences that, at least at surface level, seem to be uniformly accepted and participated in by both students and school personnel. An example of this could be drawn from school basketball games. Because of great sport rivalries and gang tensions between the different sides of Brandon city, especially the south side and the north side, high school basketball games were heavily policed at the school.

During one city game (Brandon versus North Side School) there were about 20 police officers in uniform, with guns and clubs, patrolling outside and inside the school. There were two hand-held metal detectors used on each of the students who came in the door as spectators. Some students were frisked. There were six marked police cars, one parked sideways in the parking lot cutting off traffic to the back of the school. The other police cars were parked up the hill just outside the school near, ironically, the "Welcome to Brandon High" sign. There was a paddy wagon in front of the school as well. Standing outside the paddy wagon were men, most of whom were white, in black SWAT-like uniforms. They wore shoulder pads and carried automatic weapons.

In addition, there was a helicopter circling above the school with a spotlight that bounced back and forth in the parking lot, climbed the side of the school, and returned to the parking lot, over and over again. It was very dark, but there was a lot of glare from the spotlights. The spectators were nearly all black, but there were about a dozen or so white kids. In school the next day, one teacher remarked, referring to the different skin colors of the spectators and the police, "Imagine what it would have been like to be black coming into this school last night."

How schooling can degenerate into an activity that resembles war more than education results from many factors that exist both inside and outside schools. Some reasons for the persistence of systemic violence can be found in national rhetoric that sanctions forms of discriminatory punishment and policing. One could see the evolution of systemic violence partly as an outcome of congressional backing of "three strikes" and "minimum sentencing" policies. The mass building of prisons, cutting social services for youth, greater focus on judicial measures for juveniles, prosecuting children as young as 7 as adults, and the mean-spirited call for better (read "stricter") detention facilities have trickled down to state, city, and school policymakers and emboldened them, and in some cases created pressure for them, to instate their own forms of zero tolerance. To consider this a "symbolic" form of violence, as some do, understates the real consequences of institutional practices that confine, demean, and misunderstand young people—that create in our society a general feeling that teenagers are no good, out of control, and morally void—and therefore bolster punishment in favor of pedagogy, control in favor of understanding.

INTERPERSONAL AND HIDDEN VIOLENCE

Brandon High always had a problem with the fire alarms. Every couple of weeks they were pulled. When spring arrived and during Regents testing, false alarms—along with bomb threats—caused the evacuation of the school almost daily. One day that I was there, the alarms went off three times before lunch. On one particularly cold and gloomy day in March somebody pulled the fire alarm and as was typical the halls suddenly became chaotic with the flow of students pouring out of their classrooms and into the corridors and down the steps on their way out of the school. Some students ignored teachers who urged them to go directly outside and took a moment to snatch their coats from their lockers. Some friends shared coats, draping sleeves over each other's heads, and using the coats to cushion their ears from the blaring alarm. The cold came bursting into the school as some teachers held doors open for the hundreds of students heading out.

During a false alarm, the blaring, the flickering lights, and the streams of bodies pushing through the halls and down steps cause chaos. It is difficult to speak to students even if you could get to them through the rush of bodies. In one doorway a group of students met a student in a red T-shirt and blocked his exit, and for a moment I did not know what was happening amid the commotion. I watched from a distance, while holding open a door. One boy in the group stood before the student and, looking him in the eye, bobbed back and forth in front of him—to the left, right, then left again. At first I thought they were just fooling around together, but then I noticed that the boy in the red T-shirt stood still, as if frozen, and remained quiet, looking away from the bobbing boy. A moment passed and the individual in the red T-shirt suddenly came to life and tried to walk around but his exit remained blocked as the bully scuttled in front of him. "Let me pass," the boy in the red T-shirt seemed to say, still not looking directly at the bully.

The boy in the red T-shirt wore very thick glasses. I let go of the door I was holding and moved closer to them—by now most of the students were out of the building. I noticed that the boy's left eye stared upward and to the left while the other peered forward. The bully said, "I just want to make sure you can see me." He looked into one eye and then the other, shuffling back and forth, as if he were not sure which eye was seeing him. A moment later a teacher came over and grabbed the bully by the collar, turned him around, and pointed him out the door.

The group left the building and the boy in the red T-shirt also walked out. On the way out, the teacher, who did not know what had happened and was concerned only with getting the false alarm over with, told the boy in the red T-shirt, "Hurry along, what's taking you so long?" The group of boys, the bully included, went to one side of the cement wall outside the school; a couple quickly smoked cigarettes. The student in the red T-shirt went the other way and became lost in the crowd. Wanting to avoid the group, he stood at the other end of the cement wall by himself. He huddled against himself, cold and shamed, it seemed, trying to look inconspicuous. I told the teacher what had happened and he went over to talk to the student in the red T-shirt. The student told the teacher that "they were just being jerks" and did not want to pursue the issue. He too just wanted to get the false alarm over with.

While this incident occurred in a crowded area and a teacher had attempted to attend to the problem, this is not always the case. Later that same day, after day school had let out and another false alarm had occurred, a group of girls came in late to afternoon school. They came down the main stairwell into the basement pushing each other in jest. Their laughter echoed in the nearly vacant corridor. The girls' track team was also in the basement, running laps through the hallways since it was too cold and rainy to do their practice outside.

As the group of afternoon school girls came down the stairwell, the track team—about 13 girls—came running past. As one rather large girl in spandex pants passed, a girl from the afternoon school group reached out and tried to slap her buttocks. She missed and her face showed her frustration but also her pleasure for having demonstrated her bravado in front of her friends. As the runner turned the corner down another corridor, the afternoon school girl yelled, "You better run, you bitch." Then she mumbled so that just the group would have the pleasure to hear her: "You ain't going to do nothing 'bout that fat ass." Another girl in the group said, "Fat shit."

The runners were still passing. Behind the main group of team members, a single runner with large breasts brought up the rear. The group of girls saw her and one shouted, "Shit, look at 'em tits bounce." The runner, who heard this comment, reached out as she passed and smacked the afternoon school girl in the face. The girl who had been struck grabbed the runner's halter top and bra and pulled down hard and fast, nearly yanking the runner off her feet. There was the sound of a rip, but the girl managed to hold up her clothing by crossing her arms against her chest. She stopped running, and sweating heavily, winded and furious, approached the group of girls. The girls gathered closer together, except for one who seemed to be embarrassed by the entire scene. For a moment it seemed that there was going to be a fight—this runner against the group of girls. I said something to make them notice me, something like "Why don't you chill out?" The runner looked at me, seeing me for the first time, thought twice, and in an instant turned around, yelled "fuckin' whores" (the insult of choice for many girls), and ran to catch up with her teammates.

Unlike shootings and fights—but in some ways similar to systemic violence—sexual attacks and harassment, bullying, and jumpings are hidden forms of interpersonal violence. They are not always noticed and sometimes they are the least discussed incidents in conversations about violence. Yet these incidents remain prevalent problems in schools (Besag, 1989; Katz, 1995; Stein, 1999). These are forms of violence that occur nearly every day and are at times committed outside the purview of school officials, in areas of the school that are the least populated, such as bathrooms, locker rooms, stairwells, and certain corridors, or, in the case of the track team incident, during afternoon school. One student claimed that he never used the bathroom in the school because he was afraid of being jumped in a stall. This had happened to him once. Other students wore their gym clothes under their jeans and shirts to avoid using the locker rooms. Since sport-gear clothing was so popular as school clothing, changing for gym was sometimes done just by pulling off a sweatshirt to show a T-shirt.

Ironically, though, forms of hidden violence at Brandon High were often committed in crowded areas such as hallways and outside during lunch or study halls, mostly because students who did harass felt relatively certain that school staff—while professing an intolerance of such behavior—would not ordinarily reprimand them. In these cases, hidden forms of violence occurred rather quickly and staff did not know how to respond, or were uncertain about what happened or did not see it: A boy grabbed a girl's buttocks while passing in the hallway; a group of boys pushed another boy against lockers and knocked his books out of his hands, then quickly passed; and, as in the above case, a kid with a physical difference was harassed during a false alarm. During one incident, a student quietly teased a smaller boy relentlessly about his size while on lunch line and in full view of other students and teachers.

Since bullying and harassment are "tactics to obtain power and influence" (Gellert, 1997, p. 116), most often such forms of violence occurred between students of different social status: one race against another, boys against girls, jocks versus burnouts, skinny kids mocking heavy kids, handsome kids bullying the not-so-handsome. While it is not always appropriate to examine harassment and bullying together, they are similar in that each is a means of reproducing in schools power structures that exist in society, and they are often precursors of more overt forms of hate crimes (Katz, 1995).

And yet there was a general feeling—in spite of in-service and professional development days set aside for discussing sexual harassment and bullying—that the school could not do much to deal with the problem. As one teacher explained, "There is nothing to sink your teeth into with this kind of behavior. It happens quickly, people don't really complain, so it's passed over." According to Soriano et al. (1994, p. 221), "Schools are ill prepared to intervene, much less prevent acts of hate against identified targeted groups," for several reasons, including: "(a) absence of a plan by administration, (b) lack of educator cultural awareness and sensitivity, (c) lack of parental involvement in the schools, and (d) poor teacher listening and communication skills."

But in addition to the inability and reluctance of the school to deal effectively with forms of hidden violence, there is also a reluctance on the part of some students to report harassment. Some students are afraid or do not know how; others, especially girls who are sexually harassed, feel embarrassed or believe that the administrators (who are most often men) will not or cannot do anything about the problem (see also Artz, 1998; Stein, 1995). Hence, there is fear and embarrassment for students who would rather keep their mouths shut than make a complaint that could draw attention and perhaps ridicule—this may have been the case with the boy who was bullied during the false alarm.

A counselor at Brandon High thought that sexual harassment and attacks were the least reported form of violence that occurred in the school. Another counselor added, "I think we would be shocked if we knew how often girls had to put up with meanness and sexual stuff from boys in this school." There was also the belief among some students and administrators that these forms of violence were not really "violent"—or, at the very least, were not serious enough to report (see also Waldner-Haugrud, 1995). Another reason these forms of violence remain hidden is because of the disciplinary action that is taken, especially in cases of sexual assault. As the principal explained to me in a meeting, "Anything involving sexual harassment becomes very individualized." For the good of the student and the school, administrators do not want to publicize incidents of sexual harassment, and therefore such incidents are dealt with behind closed doors.

Ultimately, then, sexual violence—unless it accompanies an outright rape—is kept hidden in multiple ways: First, it occurs in places where nobody can see or discreetly in public places; second, it is rarely reported; and finally, disciplinary action is low-profile. While stories about a shooting or a fight may become the main conversation of the day for teachers and students, sexual harassment and to some extent bullying and jumpings are rarely discussed, or noticed, and therefore are not always dealt with in schools such as Brandon High.

A GLIMPSE AT PEER MEDIATION

As mentioned earlier, forms of hidden violence are often the cause of more overt types of aggression and taunting. Bullying, harassment, and fights are part of a continuum of violence that extends from teasing to physical forms of confrontation. Brandon High had a well-regarded peer mediation program where one could gain a perspective on the types and complexities of conflicts that arose in the school. During one week, two couples—each a boy and a girl—were sent to peer mediation for fighting in school. Because the physical contact was rather mild (described as slapping, not punching), the students were not automatically suspended. Meanwhile, during their mediations the focus was on the fighting but based on what the students said, there were other, perhaps more serious, issues involved. It is worth examining one mediation in detail, for it demonstrates the complexity of some student conflicts—how fighting was often the outcome of hidden forms of violence, and how sexual harassment was often an underlying factor in fights between boys and girls.

The mediation involved two African American students. Because the usual mediation room was being used for college visits, the mediation had to be held upstairs in a room that was typically used for after-school student meetings. We entered the room and sat around the table, the adult mediator careful to separate the two disputants by sitting between them, as was customary with mediations. The student mediator, a white, blond-haired girl, sat across from the adult mediator.

Manuel had been called to mediation for fighting with Keisha and seemed somewhat reluctant to be part of the mediation. Keisha was an 11th-grader who admitted to liking and wanting to date Manuel. According to Manuel, who was not interested in Keisha, the fight occurred because Keisha did not leave him alone. She followed him, imitated him, and spread rumors about him. In the following quotation, AOMD stands for "All On My Dig," which refers to someone imitating the style and dress of another. "Jocking" has a similar meaning. "Putting out statements" refers to spreading rumors and making false complaints to teachers. Manuel claimed in the mediation:

> The problem is that Keisha is AOMD, jocking me, and then she starts making complaints, putting out statements about me—her associates and herself—statements about me and my homies. I find out that there are these statements put out about me. And she is AOMD, jocking me, and my father has to keep coming up to the school because I keep getting in trouble because of her. He was here yesterday, and now he is going to have to come up here again today. She and her associates have to learn to say "Stop" if they don't like it, me ribbing, my ribbing. They don't have a sense of humor. I'm always ribbing people.

When Manuel mentioned that he was ribbing—or teasing—Keisha and her friends, the adult mediator asked him to explain what he "ribbed" about. Manuel explained that he was only "buffing" her. Again the adult mediator wanted to know what he meant. At this point, Manuel and Keisha looked at each other. They smiled and chuckled, no longer enemies, but the main figures in a secret joke and private language. Manuel explained that buffing was like a "big wet one." The adult mediator still did not understand, so Manuel asked Keisha if she wanted to explain. Keisha did not respond, so Manuel turned to the mediator and asked, "Are you sure you won't be offended?" The adult mediator told him to go ahead and Manuel said, "It's like oral sex, buffing, a big wet one." Essentially, Manuel had been taunting her about having oral sex with him.

The adult mediator seemed perplexed for a moment and turned to the student mediator, who shrugged her shoulders and smirked. Manuel began knocking his fingers on the table. He seemed impatient but also proud to have caused such a sensation. Then the adult mediator turned to Manuel and told him that ribbing and buffing could be "crossing the line." She said, "It might be fun to you, but it can also be sexual harassment." Manuel, becoming defensive, insisted, "I know that. I know what you mean."

Making evident the way that high school girls so often accept sexual harassment, Keisha began to defend Manuel. She insisted that she sometimes could not take a joke and that perhaps Manuel was only joking with her. When the student mediator in the room asked Keisha, "What do you think will solve this problem? Is it possible to not see Manuel any more—that you two stay away from each other and don't talk to each other?" Keisha nodded, then said, "We can have a little ribbing now and then." Manuel, agitated, said, "No way. As far as I am concerned, you do not exist. I will not even look in your direction." The adult mediator asked Manuel, "Do you always rib girls?" Manuel, more agitated, said, "I don't want to be listening to those coneheads in the office always saying that I have problems with women." He said, "I love women. I came from a woman. My mother is a woman. I even rib my mother." The adult mediator, who had brought up the topic of sexual harassment, let the issue pass. Manuel began saying again, "We have to solve our own problems. My father was here yesterday, now he's going to be here again today." Angrily he said, "I won't rib her any more, I won't even talk to her."

Keisha became visibly upset whenever Manuel mentioned that he would not talk to her or see her any more. Not only did she not want to pursue the issue of sexual harassment; she told him that it was okay for him to "rib" and "buff" her but that he should not go too far. After the mediation the adult mediator seemed perplexed. She turned to me and said, "See what we deal with? This is how it is." She shook her head at me and said, "Kids just don't understand sexual harassment. Some of them don't even think it is wrong."

It seems that few people—students as well as adults—understand sexual harassment. Even when people involved were vocal about what had occurred, the stories that students told were often contradictory and convoluted, which caused some staff to quickly give up trying to understand the problem. This was often the case in peer mediation sessions (Casella, 2000). In these cases, it became quite obvious that students did not tell adults all the details of their stories: Issues involving relationships, past disputes, vulgar gestures, and secret trysts, and incidents involving friends of the disputants, were often not brought up, increasing the *hidden-ness* of the violence.

Hidden violence is not hidden to the people involved in it: The tormenting that individuals do and the anguish that their victims feel are quite real. This may have been the case with Keisha; after the peer mediation session I had asked to talk to her but she did not want to, so we will never know what really went on. As a means of detecting such violence, some schools have turned to surveillance cameras, but though cameras may document incidents they will not teach adults how to talk to students about relationships or give them the time and energy to wade through convoluted stories and confusing circumstances. Sexual harassment remains merely a whisper in schools, in spite of its occurrences, partly because talking about it also means talking about sex, relationships, and students' bodies, issues most school staff would rather avoid. Meanwhile, bullying and jumpings, as well as sexual harassment, are ongoing forms of violence that are meant to humiliate and oppress. They occur for reasons that are not completely temporal—the result of a sudden flare-up or "outburst." They are the consequences of long-brimming inequities, racial animosities, and prejudices against individuals considered inferior.

MacDonald (1996, p. 84) explained that "violent behaviors have always existed in our schools. A generation ago, the schoolyard bully was a physically intimidating individual. . . . Today, that bully may still be the 'big kid,' but he or she is just as likely to be a 'little kid' with a big knife." Unlike school shootings, where the gun is obviously in the school, it is difficult to address harassment, especially when there is so much that prevents serious action, when girls do not feel comfortable reporting their own victimization and teachers are at a loss as to how to deal with it. Sometimes it is difficult to determine the differences between harassment and horseplay—especially when the "victim" seems pleased with the attention or retaliates violently. In addition, when harassment includes the use of a sharp pencil, thumbtack, or even a heavy book used like a club, the difference between harassment and weapon violence becomes hard to determine. Furthermore, individuals are not just bullies or victims, but victims can be at times the bullies and even the biggest bullies are sometimes harassed by others—perhaps the "little kid" with the "big knife." To address hidden violence in schools is to open a can of worms. We would need to examine tense social relations that have a long history, and to discuss issues that make people uneasy—such as poverty, sex, and all forms of prejudice.

SUICIDE AND SELF-MUTILATION

Though suicide is not ordinarily considered a form of school violence, I include it here for two reasons. First, suicide may, at times, be the result of experiences and traumas associated with schooling, including those caused by systemic violence. Second, Brandon High had to contend with the aftermath of two student suicides, and according to some school personnel, the suicides deserved as much attention as any fight or weapon-related incident. During the 1996–1997 school year, two Brandon High students committed suicide. One student shot himself and the other hanged himself, and the effects on the school (both students and administrators) were still being felt during the time of my research. The students were friends, and part of a group of students who called themselves the CAWBs (the Crazy Ass White Boys).

The first suicide was Mark Fisher, whom friends described as a "regular guy"—a guy who liked sports and girls. In the fall of 1996 he borrowed his mother's car without permission and when his mother came home unexpectedly and discovered what he had done, she and Mark argued outside their house in front of Mark's friend. During the argument, Mark's mother threatened to ground him. Quite suddenly, Mark went inside the house. He went to the basement and got shells for the gun that was kept upstairs, then went upstairs, loaded the gun, and shot himself in the mouth. The school counselor who worked closely with Mark's friends and family after the suicide could not say exactly what had prompted Mark to commit suicide—to react so lethally to his mother's reprimands—but she felt sure that it had more to do with a surge of frustration and anger than any long-standing depression. She, and others, thought that if something had distracted Mark, he would not have shot himself. She remarked, "To this day I believe that had the phone rung, had somebody knocked on their door, Mark would be here today. He was really impulsive."

This impulsiveness of Mark's was noted by others as well, including his friends. According to the school social worker, many students at Brandon High, and other schools she had worked at, were impulsive and sometimes felt troubled, upset, or depressed, and in these cases the availability of a gun "ups the ante." It makes suicide that much easier and tempting. According to the general public and most researchers, suicide is the outcome of depression, frustration, family situations, drug and alcohol abuse, relationship problems, alienation, loneliness, and identity problems (Hafen & Frandsen, 1986). A society that romanticizes suicide, that creates frustration for adolescents, that often misunderstands young people, may also contribute to suicide (Noddings, 1996). But often overlooked are the anachronistic laws and frontier mentalities that make guns so available in U.S. society. In cases such as Mark's, the impulsive person, who could otherwise do less damage or be calmed by another, acts hastily, sometimes fatally, when guns become commonplace items in houses and in the street. Even if it is true that an individual will find an alternative method of suicide if a gun is not available, it is also true that the alternative method will probably not be as lethal as a gun. Slamming a door, punching a wall, or taking pills and being hospitalized could have also been Mark's reaction to his situation.

And yet the availability of guns is not the lone culprit here. The second student at Brandon High who committed suicide hanged himself, and did so deliberately and quite methodically. His suicide was quite different from Mark's. Though always very quiet, Ruben became especially quiet after Mark killed himself. He did not open up to anybody, unlike his sister, who would suddenly begin crying in class thinking about Mark. On St. Patrick's Day, 1997, without any warning and apparently for no reason (there had been no fight or argument), Ruben hanged himself from his weight bench at home. The day before, he had cleaned out his locker at school, written a suicide note, and eaten dinner with his family. A psychologist who read the suicide note suspected that Ruben may have been gay, an issue that becomes significant when we consider that, according to the Department of Health and Human Services, gay and lesbian students are two to three times more likely to attempt suicide than heterosexual adolescents and comprise up to 30% of completed youth suicides annually (cited in Friend, 1998, p. 151). St. Patrick's Day was Mark's favorite holiday and nobody saw Ruben's timing as mere coincidence. Ruben's purposeful approach to suicide was so unlike Mark's, but their acts were similar in that they shattered people in the school.

Even in 1998, Linda Evers, Ruben's counselor, felt the school was still reeling from the suicides. She noted:

> The first one was kind of contained to that group, that group of friends. When you have a second one, when the second one hit, the ripples were felt much further out. It brought up just that much more for kids. I mean we had kids just falling apart, from March to June, just devastated. It didn't really calm down until January of this year. I was afraid it would start all over again with the anniversary of Ruben's [suicide]. We came back to school and then, boom, right away it was the anniversary of Mark's death. It wasn't so much the kids who were really tight with those guys, it was more the fringe. It was all those kids who it had rippled to. I guess I don't worry as much about the kids in that core group because they were pissed at Ruben.

And just last week—that's why I was so uptight—it was the anniversary of Ruben's [suicide] and I was afraid what that would bring up with students.

Students were saddened by the deaths of Mark and Ruben, but many more students became angry with the second suicide. A school counselor explained the anger: "Because they all agreed after Mark that they would never do that to each other. They all knew what it did to everybody else and they swore they would never do that to each other again." After the second suicide the group of friends became very divided. Girls for the most part wanted to keep remembering and talking about Mark and Ruben. Boys in many ways wanted to move on. They wanted to try to forget, at least for the moment. Eventually the group dissolved. There developed some bitter feelings among them—boys were accused of being insensitive, girls were accused of being self-indulgent and harping on the suicides. Those who did not want to talk about the suicides any more or were angry with Ruben felt awkward around Mark's sister, who remained in the school. Some parents in the community vocally blamed the school for being inattentive to the two boys by not recognizing the warning signs. In the end, the suicides destroyed not only the lives of two young men, but also those of families and friends, part of a community, and relationships between people in the school.

After the suicides, the school became especially attentive to distressed students and signs of potential suicide. There were workshops and lectures during the school year about depression. While it is impossible to know the extent of suicidal behavior in schools, one school counselor at Brandon High who screened for suicidal tendencies concluded that she evaluated about 40 to 50 students a year, many of whom were then referred to C-Pep, the city psychiatric ward, for further evaluation.

In 1998, during the time of my research, there were at least three incidents involving potential suicides. In one case a student found what could have been interpreted as a suicide note in the locker of a friend. In a frenzy, the student came to the guidance area with the note and showed it to one of the counselors. Meanwhile, the friend who had apparently written the note was not in school. A panic went through the counselors' suite. The principal was informed and phone calls were made to the house of the student, to relatives' houses, and to the houses of friends, and in time it was discovered that the student was at home, though she had not answered the phone. She was also depressed, having just broken up with a boyfriend. The school notified her parents about the breakup and the note found in her locker, and the student who had found the note was permitted to go home, since she had become very upset by the situation.

In another incident, a 10th-grade girl had found out during math class that an ex-boyfriend, Antoine, had been shot and killed the previous night—an incident all too common for young black men in the city. Antoine was a former student at Brandon High. The girl was told about the killing by a friend while she was sitting in class. The teacher did not know what was going on when the student suddenly stood up, knocked over her chair, kicked her desk, and left the classroom saying she was going to "kill." The math teacher came to the guidance area and told the girl's counselor that she was not sure if the student had meant "kill herself" or "kill the person who had killed Antoine." An administrator called the student's house, but there was no answer. This time, the principal left the school to look for the girl. Later, it was discovered that the girl had not left the school, but was cutting her classes and hiding in one of the school corridors, not talking to anyone.

Another situation involved a student by the name of Monica. Monica was a small girl, white, who dressed in "goth" black and wore on most days black lipstick and white face powder. She was in ninth grade. She had lived at Wordsworth House, a shelter for homeless and runaway girls, and did not get along with her parents, who had to some extent "disowned" her. In time, Monica was kicked out of Wordsworth House for breaking curfew rules. Meanwhile, because her parents were very religious—Monica's mother was the daughter of missionaries—Monica was also very naive about her sexuality. Her parents did not speak to her about sex and did not permit her to participate in the sex education classes offered by Brandon High through the health program. Until recently, Monica did not know how girls got pregnant. Her boyfriend had herpes and she did not know what the disease was or how people got it. In time, other girls explained this to her, but she continued to have unprotected sex with the boy.

During the year, Monica had cut her wrists superficially with a kitchen knife. On another occasion, with a red pen she drew severed veins on the underside of her forearms. She had also come to school one day with a deep burn on her wrist, which she said was made with a cigarette—though she would not say if she had done it to herself or if somebody had done it to her. In response, an assistant principal tried to have Monica admitted to C-Pep for evaluation, but the psychiatric ward refused to take her because she did not have the appropriate insurance. An administrator at C-Pep assured the school that they had already evaluated Monica (the year before) and had prescribed medication for her, which she refused to take. There was nothing else they could do, they claimed.

During the next week, Monica went through the school days as an outsider, if she came to school at all. As one of only a handful of goth students, and the only one in ninth grade, she seemed friendless and lonely. She walked in the hallways as if she were trying to melt into the cinderblock walls. One day, Monica came into school very withdrawn and perhaps high on marijuana or a bit drunk. She had not slept in two days and had been eating only candy bars. One pocket bulged with the crumpled wrappers of Snickers and Mars Bars. School administrators tried to take her home, but her family suggested that they take her to her uncle's house. At her uncle's house, Monica did not want to sleep. She was exhausted but complained that she would die if she fell asleep. Her uncle emphasized to the administrator that Monica could stay only a couple of days.

Monica was supposed to call the school the following morning, but by noon she still had not called. An administrator explained in a positive fashion that the principal was going to suspend Monica for coming into school high, that she would have to have a Superintendent's Hearing, and that she would most likely be expelled from school. She was, according to the administrator, "out of control." While her circumstances were different from those involving a school fight, the disciplinary action taken against her was identical to that which occurred when students fought: Superintendent's Hearing and expulsion. Too often, school discipline policies did not leave room for administrators to consider the uniqueness of cases: Whether one was suicidal or a fighter, the school's response could be the same.

In addition to depression, alienation, and other causes, there is also a certain amount of inattentiveness and lack of caring that contributes to suicide. In many ways, adults have given up on delinquent and poor children and the social system aimed at helping them: In the words of the C-Pep worker, "There is nothing we can do." One day after school, in a conference room, a group of staff members sat and shook their heads, finishing their coffee, while talking about Monica. One assistant principal figured that Monica was going to drop out of school—that she probably would not even attend the judicial hearing. A school counselor worried that Monica would end up killing herself and wanted to call C-Pep again. Another administrator said that Monica would probably end up squatting with other runaways in an abandoned building. The south side was full of these abandoned buildings, remnants of the city's factory-filled past. Given the fact that Monica was working sporadically labeling envelopes at night on the north side of the city, one administrator felt that she would be "certainly victimized" taking the bus at night. It seemed that many administrators could foresee Monica's future but felt incapable of doing anything about it.

Because suicides are sometimes not reported as suicides (in order to avoid the stigma associated with them), it is difficult to say how many young people kill themselves. Some estimates suggest that about 5,000 youth commit suicide each year, and that for every successful suicide there may be as many as 50 to 150 attempts (Guetzloe, 1989; Marcus, 1996). That boys kill themselves and girls "threaten" to kill themselves—as was the case at Brandon High—is typical of suicide as well. According to the National Center for Education Statistics [NCES] (1995), for individuals between the ages of 15 and 24, the suicide rate (number of suicides per 100,000 individuals) for white boys jumped from 8.6 to 22.7 between 1988 and 1992. African American boys have had the greatest increase: 4.1 to 18.0. For white females the numbers were lower: 2.3 to 3.8. African American girls have the lowest rate of suicide: less than .05 to 2.2.

For homosexual students, the numbers are even more startling: Suicide is the leading cause of death for gay and lesbian students, and according to a 1991 study of 137 gay and bisexual male youth, 30% had attempted suicide once and 13% reported multiple attempts (cited in Friend, 1998, p. 151). That the suicidal students at Brandon High—Mark, Ruben, and the girls who threatened suicide (with the exception of one)—were white and one may have been gay is quite typical. White students in general commit suicide more frequently than students of color. In discussions, African American students sometimes criticized white students for suicide the way that white students criticized black students for city shootings. But viewed from a different perspective, shootings of African Americans by African Americans can be seen as an outcome of self-hatred and not so unlike suicide—perhaps a form of what Marcus (1996) referred to as "indirect suicide."

While it is not always appropriate to examine suicide and violence against others together, some research suggests that suicide and homicide are, in a sense, two sides of the same coin. Short (1997, p. 135) noted that "structural and cultural conditions that produce the externalization of blame provide a rationale for striking out against those who are blamed—resulting, in extreme form, in homicide. Conversely, when blame is internalized in individuals (that is, attribution of failure or loss is to the self), the result, in extreme form, is suicide." For those who view violence as a response to frustration, blame for the frustration is a factor in determining how a person will react.

When discussing suicide or other forms of violence, it is important to see beyond the aggressive individual, to recognize how society causes unnecessary frustration, how institutions can be violent themselves, and how violence is often both a cause and an outcome of pain. According to some students, adults put too many pressures on them. They are forced to achieve, to conform, to perform, to follow in particular footsteps, to be like adults when they are not adults, and to accept adult responsibilities when they are already accepting and attempting to cope with adolescent responsibilities. And it is not only adults who cause such pressures. Other adolescents as well can be cruel, even to their friends. When I watched interactions in hallways between students, it often seemed that some adolescents were masters of "hurting." More than anything, they knew how to tear each other apart with the most subtle of "weapons"—ignoring others, using body language, spreading rumors, or using vicious language. But I saw another side as well. As I began to recognize suicide as a form of violence, I often wandered the halls of Brandon High seeing beyond the everyday apparent conflicts and wondered which students had attempted suicide, who was contemplating it, and who would be contemplating it in the future. Behind the facades, the clothing, the makeup, the cheery or bored faces, students themselves admitted that there lie within them feelings of depression, loneliness, and self-hatred. Ultimately, suicide—and what could be interpreted as indirect suicide—was an unnerving form of self-violence that had real consequences at Brandon High: unnerving for the apparent inability of adults to comprehend it, to recognize the warning signs, or to do anything about it.

THE SPECTACLE OF VIOLENCE

While the circumstances involving Monica and the cases of hidden violence may suggest that Brandon High was not or could not be responsive to some incidents of violence, in other ways the school spent much time addressing violence in the building. As mentioned earlier, Federal legislation in the 1990s made available great sums of money for schools such as Brandon High to develop peer mediation programs, to hire police officers, to develop citywide partnerships, and to form conflict resolution programs. Brandon High's development of a peer mediation program, its liaisons with the police department, and its move to hire security guards were partly an outcome of these new policies, which, through no coincidence, occurred at a time of increased development and marketing of conflict resolution and violence-prevention programs and curricula. The incorporation of these changes often entailed large sums of money, schedule changes, training, and, it was hoped, a new school ethos. But in the everyday running of the school, less distinguishable responses to violence were enacted. Sometimes these responses amplified the problem.

At Brandon High, responses to violence were often exaggerated and sometimes represented the folly, paranoia, and fears that the threat of violence spurred in schools. It could cause school staff to battle the imaginary at the expense of the real. For example, toward the end of the school year, the administration staged a drill meant to prepare the students for a crisis involving a gunman in the school. The drill was called the "Mr. Panther drill"—the panther was Brandon High's mascot—and was conducted on a day I was in the school observing DARE classes. I was taking a break from my observations when an assistant principal approached me and told me that I should be ready at 1:30 for a new drill. I wasn't sure what he meant, but finished my lunch in the school cafeteria while talking to some students, then went to the main office just before 1:30. At 1:30 an office secretary made an announcement over the school PA system: "Mr. Panther, please report to the auditorium foyer." The assistant principal explained to me that "Mr. Panther" was code to let all staff know that there was a gunman in the school. The "report to the auditorium foyer" indicated that the gunman was in the auditorium foyer. This was meant to be standard code in the case of a real emergency.

Once this announcement was made, teachers were required to usher all students into their classrooms and to lock their doors, which some tried to do. In general, students did not know about the drill but most school personnel did. Those students who were out in the hallways and were called into classrooms where they did not belong seemed confused. Humorously, one asked if the teacher wanted him to be a guest speaker. The rest of the communication between administrators and the school police officer was conducted through walkie-talkies. First, the school police officer was called to the scene of the "shooting." Detective O'Hara came trotting down the hallway with a walkie-talkie in one hand, his other hand holding his holster so that his gun would not slap against his hip while he ran. Then the school nurse was called because there "was a student down." She appeared with a white first aid kit and went directly to the foyer, walking very quickly. Then a mock city emergency unit was called, and finally, all staff who knew CPR were asked to report to the foyer.

The drill lasted about 30 minutes and was filled with confusion and mistakes. Some students continued to roam the halls during the drill and did not know what was going on. Some thought the drill was related to bomb threats the school had been receiving (during the previous week, there had been five bomb scares). Some teachers did not participate and it was noted by the social worker who had watched that the nurse might have been shot if she reported to the foyer without any form of backup. When teachers who knew CPR were called to the scene, over 20 teachers arrived.

This Mr. Panther spectacle had the effect not of preparing the school for a crisis but of making evident how misguided notions about violence in schools sometimes are. Essentially, the school prepared for a form of violence that was unlikely to happen while shifting focus away from violence that already existed. The seriousness of gun violence cannot be overstated, especially during the 1997–1999 school years when tensions were very high because of tragedies involving multiple killings at schools in the United States. But fears of gun violence, the feeling among administrators that they had to do something to prepare for violence, and a culture that had already seen the use of "duck and cover" drills were the real impetuses of the spectacle. Whether a Mr. Panther drill could ever prepare a school for an armed gunman is questionable, but such drills are becoming more common in schools. They are an example of how adults deflect attention away from more effective violence-prevention activities in favor of those that are either "crisis management" or, as noted earlier, punitive in nature.

Another example of this deflection of attention involved the Crisis Intervention Team (CIT) at the school. The CIT was made up of administrators, teachers, and counselors, and was developed in response to the two student suicides. Originally, the focus of the team was to help students through periods of "grief and loss." When the CIT was developed, its members counseled the friends of the two Brandon High suicide victims, and since then had helped students who were depressed or suffering from personal losses. With 1,400 students in the school, incidents involving grief and loss were common and it was admirable that the school had developed a responsive committee.

Ultimately, though, in 1998, the focus of the CIT shifted from "grief and loss" to "crisis management." In one meeting, the school psychologist led the group with a plan for how the team should respond to a shooting in the school. It focused not on helping students with grief and loss but on tactics that should be used in the event of a shooting and recommendations to have more "mock trial runs" such as the Mr. Panther drill. In the last meeting of the year, the chair of the CIT invited an intake counselor from C-Pep to discuss how to evaluate students with emotional traumas; ultimately, though, the meeting was about how teachers and administrators should respond to a killing in the building. Though unqualified to do so, the C-Pep counselor discussed the importance of getting federal aid to buy security equipment. A teacher wanted to know if there was money to hire another police officer. In spite of the original intentions, the CIT turned into a committee that hyped security and redirected conversations away from already existing problems of hidden violence, depression, and grief and loss in the school.

A PORTRAIT OF A SCHOOL

My description of Brandon High does not do justice to the entire school. There was much going on there that was not violent, that was productive, educative, and caring in nature. Most staff were well-intentioned and skilled educators. Most students felt safe and none really considered gun violence the immediate problem. But many were concerned about the great number of fights in the hallways and the cafeteria. Sometimes feelings of danger came from unexpected sources. When asked when they felt unsafe in school, some students remarked that they felt in most danger during the bomb threats. During the last 3 months of the school year in 1998, there were over 15 bomb threats called into the school, a fact that caused great anxiety, especially as the week-long State Regents tests approached.

Some students said that they did not feel safe when there was a fight because students gathering around the fight were dangerous themselves. One student was afraid to come to school because he owed money to some-body who threatened to jump him if he did not pay. Those who did worry about gun violence expressed greater fear of their neighborhoods than their school; in fact, most schools are safer than their surrounding communities (Goldstein, Harootunian, & Conoley, 1994; Prothrow-Stith, 1991). Teach-ers and staff had similar reactions. Though their talk about gun violence at times ended with a kind of tongue-in-cheek "Well you never know," most considered the school safe. They worried more about fighting, suicide, and family abuse than forms of weapon violence occurring in the school. School personnel recognized these other problems, yet felt that they had little time to address them: "I have enough to do without being kids' par-ents" was a common refrain. Referring to the demanding schedule of a teacher, and the expectations that are put on them, one wanted to know, "Where do I get the time to not only educate these kids but also to raise them?"

It is difficult to capture the complexity of a school, and this holds true when examining a school through the lens of violence. As I have tried to demonstrate here, the problem exists on many levels. On one level, school violence is more a *response* to violence, a systemic sparring with students. It includes discipline policies, new committees, and programs meant to eradicate violence that sometimes bolster forms of systemic violence. On another level, school violence is an ongoing and somewhat underground problem that entails forms of verbal and physical harassment, bullying, jumpings, and self-destructive behavior.

If we were to shift our focus a bit we would also notice that school violence at Brandon High became a "commonsense" part of the day, with a mutual understanding between individuals that it is inevitable. This inevi-tability was expressed in offhand remarks about "another fight in the lunchroom" and the presence of personnel, including hall monitors, assis-tant principals, and police officers, who were charged with the task of school control. Nobody seemed to think much about the use of walkie-talkies, metal detectors, guns (carried by the school police officer and the DARE teacher), and other security devices in school. These accessories are seen as necessary and in time as natural components of a school building. When I first entered Brandon High I was taken aback by all this antiviolence technology. This was not school as I had experienced it as an adolescent. But in time, I too—who early in the year had gone home with headaches because of the incessant static of walkie-talkies—did not notice the equipment as much, for it seemed to melt into the everyday running of things.

This portrait of Brandon High is meant to set the stage for a closer look at violence and responses to violence in school. But this closer look must occur at the same time as we consider policies of the 1990s that shaped state and citywide responses to the problem. These were policies that made way for zero tolerance, school judicial and screening committees, liaisons with the police, and new connections with nonprofit organizations and the criminal justice system. This loose assortment of institutions is, in many ways, the complete school system. It represents the reaches of schooling in all of its social service, judicial, and community characteristics. It points, as well, not only to the interpersonal qualities of violence but also to its political features at state and city levels. The actions that took place in Brandon High, while a direct response to and outcome of rising incidents of violence and perceived violence in the building, were also reflections of public policy and were shaped by politics and urban relations. These are issues that will be explored in the following chapters.

CHAPTER 3

The Screening Committee and the Prison Track

In May 1996, Dennis Vacco, the New York State Attorney General, released a study called *Report on Juvenile Crime* (Juvenile Justice Commission, 1996). The report was prepared by an ad hoc committee comprised of members of the New York State Department of Education, university professors and researchers, district attorneys and judges, representatives from school boards, and others deemed experts on juvenile and school violence. Prior to publication of the report, the commission organized the Rochester Roundtable Summit. In Rochester, New York, the commission had a formal meeting to prepare plans for public hearings about juvenile and school violence in New York State.

In 1996, public hearings were held in a number of cities around the state, including Brandon city, to assess community concerns regarding juvenile crime and to discuss solutions to problems of violence. *Report on Juvenile Crime* was based on statements and testimony that resulted from these roundtable sessions and public hearings. The commission's findings, as noted in the report, were grim, and the overall tone was one of alarm.

The report began with a general warning, using language and even expressions—the "rising tide"—that were reminiscent of another report that had gained much public attention in the 1980s, *A Nation at Risk: The Imperative for Educational Reform*, submitted by the National Commission on Excellence in Education. *A Nation at Risk* (1983, p. 1) appeared during the Ronald Reagan and William Bennett years, and became famous (or infamous) for noting "the rising tide of mediocrity" in U.S. public schools. Using the same language, in its opening sentence *Report on Juvenile Crime* bemoaned the rising tide of violence in New York schools:

> New York has been devastated by the rising tide of youth violence. Today, in New York State, juveniles are committing acts of violence on our streets, in our neighborhoods, and in our schools, at record levels. One cannot open a newspaper or turn on a television without seeing horrible stories about kids

murdering kids, students stabbing teachers, schools armed with metal detectors, and frustrated law enforcement officials and judges who can do little about it. (Juvenile Justice Commission, 1996, p. 2)

The report continued by noting federal statistics that demonstrated this rising tide of youth violence: that the number of juvenile homicide offenders tripled between 1984 and 1994; that New York was among the top five states with the highest juvenile violent crime arrest rates; and that if trends continued, juvenile arrests for violent crime would more than double by the year 2010 (Juvenile Justice Commission, 1996, p. 2). While some of the initiatives and suggestions stated in the report were quite appropriate and nonthreatening, the general intonation was bleak and suggestions for reform were almost entirely punitive. In its conclusion, the report recommended several legislative initiatives:

1. Fingerprint and photograph all juvenile felons.
2. Increase prison sentences for juvenile felons.
3. Automatic transfer of Family Court juvenile records.
4. Automatically share juvenile Family Court information with schools and appropriate agencies.
5. Forfeit youthful-offender status on a second felony conviction.
6. Authorize Family Court search and arrest warrants.
7. Stop the speedy trial clock if a juvenile fails to appear in court.
8. Hold parents accountable in Family Court by requiring restitution, family treatment, and counseling.
9. Establish gun-free school zones.

The last initiative, "establish gun-free school zones," reflected the federal 1990 Gun-Free School Zones Act (PL 101-649) and was presented as a New York State bill as the School Zone Violence Prevention Act (No. 02-96). It prohibited the possession of a firearm on a school bus or within 1,000 feet of a school, college, university, or municipal playground. Exceptions were granted in the case that a municipality or school requested an armed presence, as was the case at Brandon High in regard to the school's armed police officer and DARE teacher.

Reflecting national trends, the report both mimicked and ushered in the federal "get tough on crime" and "three strikes" mentality in New York State schools. Like the federal Gun-Free Schools Act of 1994 (PL 103-227), which gave fruition to zero tolerance, the report coincided with rising general support for more severe penalties for unruly and violent students and more militant forms of discipline, including school policing and greater use of suspension and expulsion of students. During the 1997–1998 school year in the United States, 3,930 students were expelled under a zero-tolerance policy; almost half of these students (43%) were referred to an alternative school or program for violent offenders, such as Brandon city's TAIP school (Sinclair, 1999).

The focus of this chapter is on Brandon High's screening committee, which determined the placements of recently suspended and expelled students, many of whom had been in fights, suicidal, or involved in other forms of violence described in the previous chapter. While some have questioned the constitutionality of suspensions and expulsions and have criticized the discrimination involved in these procedures, what is often neglected in research and other commentary is the means by which students are reinstated in the school. There is a general belief that once a student has been suspended or expelled, and all has been done according to due process and appropriate school policy, students' reinstatement ends the punishment. Unfortunately, suspension and expulsion do not end with the tenure of the sentence. At Brandon High, as at other high schools, students had to sign a probationary contract and go before a committee—sometimes called the "screening board," sometimes the "reinstatement committee," and at Brandon High, the "screening committee"—that determined students' school placements after being forced out.

GOING BEFORE THE SCREENING COMMITTEE

At Brandon High, the screening committee was made up of a guidance counselor, the special education teacher (who was also director of the afternoon school program), an assistant principal, and, at times, a teacher from the afternoon school program. The primary purpose of the screening committee was to interview students who had recently been suspended or expelled, or who were transferring in from other schools. Some students came before the committee for reasons other than those associated with violence. Some had dropped out and wanted to be reinstated; some were merely new to the district; many had complicated but presumably innocent stories about general transience with multiple residential moves (living with aunts, uncles, and cousins) and needed to be admitted to a school in their new district (see Tucker, Marx, & Long, 1998). Most of the students who came before the screening committee were poor and most were African American; many of the girls had children, and some of the boys had been incarcerated or had attended some form of boot camp. Some students came to meetings alone; others came with parents, guardians, social workers, or parole officers.

The screening committee met each Thursday from 2:00 to 4:00, though at times they either ended earlier or continued until almost 6:00.

Usually, the committee saw between six and eight students each Thursday. Most of the screenings took place in the conference room off the main office, though at times they had to be held in the meeting room in the guidance office when the main conference room was being used for other purposes. The guidance office meeting room was used primarily for university and college visiting days, which occurred almost daily during the end of the school year—though students who came before the screening committee rarely participated in them.

The unsaid truth about the screening committee was that it steered students to the afternoon school program and did so in sometimes unjust ways but also in ways seen by the committee as necessary in order to preserve safety and control in the building. The screening committee was in many ways a function of the afternoon school. James Maddy, who was both a member of the screening committee and director of the afternoon school program, explained that "the afternoon school program is meant for nontraditional students who cannot succeed in day school. It is like the old night schools." Students who came before the screening committee were considered, at best, "nontraditional," and therefore prime candidates for the program.

Officially, there were about 400 students in afternoon school—nearly a third of the total 1,400 students at Brandon High—in three different programs, including the Occupational Learning Center (OLC), the Evening Learning Department Program (ELDP), and the General Education Diploma (GED) program. OLC was a technical education program that included as its primary function the placement of students at Central Tech (the local vocational school). ELDP was for students who could not attend day school because of work, children, or fears associated with gangs. They took one class subject each day from 3:00 to 5:30 and in 3 years fulfilled the requirements to receive a standard high school diploma. The GED program was a series of preparation classes for students to pass the GED test and to receive a GED high school diploma. As noted earlier, students in afternoon school spent their time working individually on packets, or sometimes in groups, and teachers did not teach so much as supervise them. A somewhat more loosely connected part of the afternoon school program was the job developer, who came to the school each week to help afternoon school students find jobs.

The following are brief vignettes taken from field notes of four screening committee meetings. There is no true way to capture in narrative the complexities of life and school experiences, but the incidents involved in these cases do highlight the major themes that emerged in most meetings and in some ways, then, represent typical sessions between students and the committee. Between each of the cases I make comments but save more discussion until after all of the examples have been presented.

The race, social class, and gender of the students involved in each of the cases reflect the general composition of the students who went before the committee: All four were working-class or poor, two were male, two were female, and all but one African American. The cases show the variety of circumstances that must be dealt with by school staff, and highlight a difficult balancing act: how to uphold the rights of deeply troubled young people at the same time that we protect individuals in school from students who are potentially dangerous to themselves or others.

CASE I

The first meeting of the day was strange and heartbreaking. Jamil was 16 years old and had 2 ½ school credits. He wanted to stay in day school but the committee would not allow it. He arrived with his mother and sat at the conference table with the committee. Both were African American, the mother about 40 years old. As was typical, James Maddy explained the purpose of the committee to Jamil and his mother: that it was an impartial group, a formal meeting, intended to determine the placement of incoming students. Mr. Maddy asked Jamil to say something about himself: "Tell us about Jamil," he said. Jamil shrugged his shoulders. He was grinning and seemed nervous. He was well known to the school administration as a kind of class clown. He was handsome, thin, his hair in tight, long dreads. He sat at the table as if excited by the attention, darting his eyes at each member.

Linda Evers, a counselor and a member of the committee, looked at Jamil's school records and noted that he had cut a lot of classes: "You missed 31 classes of biology," she said. As if Jamil were not in the room, Mr. Maddy explained, "Jamil's not the type of kid to not come to school—he did come to school, he just did not go to classes." The mother asked Mr. Maddy, "So where is he when he skips classes?" Mr. Maddy said that he just wanders the hall, he's "one of those kids, a hall wanderer." Mr. Maddy asked Jamil, "So where are you when you miss biology?" Jamil shrugged his shoulders and said, "in the cafeteria." Mr. Maddy said that he has also been seen in Evergreen (a nearby park where some students go during lunch or to hang out after school). Jamil insisted that he did not go there—that he usually just went to the cafeteria.

For a moment, the mother seemed emboldened and angry. She asked, "So he can come to school and skip a class 31 times, and nobody says anything?" As in all cases when a parent expressed a legitimate and serious concern that implicated the school, Mr. Maddy approached the question cautiously, yet sternly and confidently. "I hear your question," he said, "but what I really think you are asking is, 'How come we didn't notify you that he had missed class so often?'" The mother nodded. Mr. Maddy said, "We should have notified you. That should have happened. But Jamil should also be in class."

Larry Ryan, an assistant principal who was also on the committee, interrupted and said rather defensively to the mother, "We have 1,300 students in this school. There is no way we can keep tabs on all of these students. It is the students' responsibility to go to class." Mr. Maddy nodded. The mother kept quiet and seemed to sink inside herself. Mr. Maddy asked Jamil why he skipped biology class. Jamil said emphatically that he did not like the teacher. He said that he wanted to stay in the day school but wanted to be transferred to another biology class. Suddenly, Mr. Maddy left the room to get Brian Arena, the assistant principal who had referred Jamil to the screening. Mr. Arena came into the room and closed the door behind him. He said that Jamil should be in the afternoon school program. Rather angrily he said that Jamil was "out of control," did not do any work, did not go to any classes, and had been reprimanded for this several times. "I myself have taken you aside and have spoken to you," Mr. Arena said. He brought up a recent incident—the one that led to his being referred to the screening: "What happened yesterday? I told you to meet me in the office and when I get there, where were you? You didn't obey." Jamil told him that he had come to the office, and had even left him a note. This surprised Mr. Arena; he had not known this. He said, "That doesn't matter. You should have waited for me. That's what most students do."

Again, Mr. Arena said that Jamil should be in the afternoon school program. Jamil insisted that he wanted to stay in day school. Angrily, Mr. Maddy asked, "Why would you want to stay in day school? As it is, you don't come now." Mr. Maddy explained the "cut-offs"—with only 2 ½ credits, he was too old to be in the ninth grade. He said, "This is a wake-up call. Perhaps if you do well in the afternoon school, really push yourself, you can get into the day school again in September." Jamil shook his head. Linda Evers shuffled some papers over to Mr. Maddy—presumably Jamil's school records—and Mr. Maddy examined them for a moment. Mr. Ryan glanced at his watch and reminded the group that they had a long list of appointments and that a snowstorm had been forecast.

The mother suddenly interrupted, shocking us all, "You see, the problems started a while ago. He was a good boy. He is a twin and his twin is missing and that's when all the trouble began, when he was 12 years old, and his twin went missing." We were all quiet for a moment. Jamil became very agitated and began smiling and crying at the same time. He put his head down on the table. Mr. Maddy asked Jamil, "Are you dizzy?" Then the mother turned to Mr. Maddy and said, "His acting-out started when his twin went missing." Mr. Maddy took a deep breath and said, "So your brother is missing." The mother said, "Sister." Mr. Maddy said, wearily, "Twin sister." He asked Jamil, "Do you want to see a counselor?" Jamil shook his head, smiling, crying. Mr. Maddy said, "Let me ask you this. Is it because you won't be a *man* if you see a counselor?" Jamil did not answer him. The mother said, "He can see my therapist. We can do that."

The adults around the table looked at each other. Jamil picked up his head and wiped his face. Larry Ryan explained to Jamil that there were advantages to afternoon school. Jamil took a deep breath and said again, "I ain't going to afternoon school. I don't want to go there." Mr. Ryan repeated, "There are advantages to afternoon school." He made Jamil guess what they were. "Guess," he said. "What do you think the advantages are?" Jamil shrugged his shoulders. "No. I want you to guess," Mr. Ryan said. "It's important. What do you think?" Jamil shrugged his shoulders again. Mr. Ryan said, "I'll give you a hint. It is quiet, there are many students like you." Jamil shrugged his shoulders. Mr. Ryan said, "You can get work done there. There are few distractions." Jamil said, "I want to stay in day school." Ms. Evers too pushed for the afternoon school and recommended that he see the job developer in order to obtain a day job. Jamil told her, "I already have a day job."

The mother interrupted and mentioned that his work hours at a local fast food restaurant had been cut because he had been in a fight at work when gang members from the north side of the city came to hassle him. Jamil had been arrested for disorderly conduct and had a date to appear in city court. Mr. Ryan seemed to be losing patience. "Jamil, why do you even want to go to school?" he asked. This is a question that Mr. Ryan asks many of the students. Jamil shrugged his shoulders. It was obvious that Jamil did not like Mr. Ryan and was refusing to answer any of his questions. Speaking to nobody in particular, Jamil said, "I want to stay in school."

Mr. Maddy turned to Jamil's mother and said, "Let's ask the mother. What do you think of all this?" The mother said, "I want him to stay in school." Mr. Maddy said, "The afternoon school." The mother, uncertainly, nodded. Jamil shook his head, defeatedly. There was nobody on his side. He said, again, "I want to stay in the *day* school." Mr. Ryan told him that he did not have a choice. He said, "You can still go to college from the afternoon school," and Jamil said, "I don't want to go to college." Ms. Evers slid the contract in front of him. In order for a student to be pulled out of day school, both a parent and the student had to sign a contract. Jamil refused to sign it. The mother signed it. Then, hesitating, Jamil signed it. Ms. Evers told him that she could give him information about Central Tech. "And remember, Jamil, you have to return your school books." Mr. Maddy told him that he could start afternoon school the following day.

After the meeting, both Mr. Maddy and Ms. Evers expressed their frustration with Jamil. Ms. Evers said, "How could he think he could stay in day school with 2 ½ credits? And he's been arrested now!" She shook her head. Mr. Maddy said, "It was her," pointing to where the mother was sitting, "that was frustrating me." I asked him why, and he explained, "I like the family members to support us. If the family member supports us, it makes the job a lot easier." Ms. Evers said, "I'm sick of seeing black males in here. There is really a problem. I'm tired of seeing black males all screwed up. Something is going to happen. There's going to be a revolution or something."

Jamil did not come to the screening committee meeting as an anonymous student. He was already known by school staff and what was known about him was not good. Staff had information on him, from class records to knowledge of his apparent presence in Evergreen Park. And this did not bode well for him. Add to this the determination of the committee to put him in the afternoon school program, that his meeting with the board must be rushed because of an approaching snowstorm, that he did not know the professional courtesies to follow in a school meeting, that he started out the meeting by acting clownish and therefore angered the adults in the room who assumed that he was not taking the meeting seriously, that he had been devastated by the disappearance of his twin sister—all this and more point to the fact that Jamil did not have a chance to stay in day school from the moment he entered the room.

Jamil was talked about as if he were not there. He was treated as just a body to be moved into afternoon school, and that movement was accomplished through the use of school records, some misleading questions, and pressure to gain the compliance and signature of his mother. Due process did not protect the student; it secured his placement with a quick signature that for Jamil represented his mother's turning on him in spite of her initial support. Ms. Evers's final comment, after the meeting was over, was a blunt way of indicating how typical the meeting was—for her, it was another screwed-up black guy. For Jamil, he was a kid who needed help (and he knew this), a school to work with him, a school that would let him transfer into another biology class—something another student, in different circumstances, would have received. Jamil was a deeply troubled kid who would no doubt pose real challenges for an already stressed school. School staff knew this, and in the end he was shucked off to afternoon school, the last thing in the world he wanted, but it made sense for an overburdened school that did not really want him.

As noted earlier, though not all screening committee meetings involved African American boys, most did. In the following vignette, however, we get to know the circumstances of a 16-year-old white girl, whose angry attitude and urban accent (and apparent speech impediment) show her as a different kind of student: She is a race traitor, white trash. As with Jamil, her meeting with the committee starts off badly and gets worse. Where Jamil had to contend with a snowstorm, Jessica gets confused, and ultimately pays the price, when the screening committee switches rooms without notifying the secretary.

CASE II

While we were waiting for the screening committee to meet, there was a commotion in the guidance area. Janice Street, the principal, came down from the main office, went into Ms. Evers's office, and closed the door. There they met with a student who had told a friend during the day that she was going to kill herself. An assistant principal came into the screening committee meeting and asked the group to move to another room so that school staff could meet with the parents of the student. The group moved into the guidance office meeting room. Ms. Evers came to the screening committee meeting late, slightly discombobulated from her meeting with the student and her parents.

Before Ms. Evers arrived, the group had been sitting around the table discussing a bomb threat that had been called into the school that morning, noting the district's new decision to buy "caller identification" telephones to curb the threats. The screening committee meetings should have started but nobody knew where the committee had moved to when it left the main conference room. The committee was talking about these new phones when they were interrupted. The conference room door opened, and a student scheduled for a meeting was ushered in by the guidance secretary. The secretary remarked that Jessica, the student, had been waiting for some time, since the secretary did not know that the group had switched rooms.

Jessica arrived with her caseworker. She came into the room, found a seat, and dropped herself into it. She kept her parka on, buried her hands deep in the pockets, and half-covered her young face with the large, snow-wet hood. She looked only at the tabletop, a spot about 6 inches from her chin. Her caseworker sat next to her. She was a white woman, about 30, who, after sitting promptly, displayed a pen and pad and seemed ready to take notes. Jessica did not look at any of us and appeared very angry.

Jessica had been a student at Brandon High but had dropped out the year before. Stories were mixed: Administrators said that she had dropped out after getting into a fight and being threatened with expulsion by the principal. Jessica claimed that she had been pregnant and had had a difficult pregnancy, which had forced her to leave.

Ms. Evers began the screening committee session by telling Jessica that the committee was "here to help you choose the best program at Brandon." She barely got through her next sentence when the PA speaker came on making an announcement about volleyball and cheerleading practice. The PA was especially loud in the guidance meeting room.

After the announcement, Mr. Maddy spoke: "We are designed to assess your background and on the basis of this information, assess your suitability for a program at Brandon." Jessica remained quiet, staring at the tabletop. Mr. Maddy asked her if she had any daycare for her son and she mumbled, "I'm finding some." Mr. Maddy nodded, then asked, "Do you work?" She said that she worked at Burger King. Jessica then looked at the clock and said, "I have to get going. I have to get to work." This seemed to annoy Mr. Maddy. He asked her when she had to be at work and she said, "Soon, and I have to catch the bus." Mr. Maddy sat back in his chair and asked her where she caught the bus. Jessica told him. He then asked her what time she finished work and Jessica told him "around midnight." He asked her how she got home at night and Jessica, becoming angry again, told him, "I have to hurry! I have work!" Mr. Maddy leaned forward and told her, "The process takes time. You need to understand that." He asked for Jessica's file, and after shuffling through papers for a moment, noticed that Jessica had been labeled with a speech impediment. He asked her, "You've worked with a speech therapist, haven't you?" Jessica nodded.

Mr. Maddy told her that she could enter the OLC program in afternoon school, but Jessica told him that she could not come to school in the afternoon because of her job. She wanted to get into Central Tech, but said that there were no openings for "nails" (manicuring). Mr. Maddy recommended the OLC program again. Jessica became annoyed and said, "Why should I take a program I'm not interested in!" The caseworker, who had been quiet up to this point, turned to Jessica and reprimanded her lightly: "What the gentleman is saying, Jessica, is that the OLC may be better suited for your schedule." Again, Jessica said, "Why should I take a program that I'm not interested in? And it *doesn't* fit into my schedule."

At this point, Larry Ryan came into the room and apologized for being late. He had been meeting with the student who had threatened suicide. There was no room for him at the table in the cramped office, so he sat in a plastic chair behind Jessica. For the next 5 minutes, Mr. Maddy, Ms. Evers, and the caseworker discussed possibilities for Jessica. They discussed her going to JVC (Job and Vocational Center, the adult education program) or the Alternative School, and that the caseworker should find out if there were other openings beside "nails" at Central Tech. Jessica interrupted them twice, each time saying, "I have to be interested in the programs. I want to be in school." As if not hearing, Mr. Maddy turned to Jessica and said, "You can be accepted into the OLC program. Who will babysit for you?" Jessica said she was working on daycare but that there was already a waiting list of 900 people for TAP (Tuition Assistance Program) funding.

Mr. Maddy sternly told Jessica about the attendance policy at Brandon. He asked her, "What time do you wake up in the morning?" She told him, "Around 9:00 or 10:00." Mr. Maddy explained, "At Brandon day school we start at 8:00. Many students leave about 1:00, and afternoon school begins at 3:00. Can you handle that?" Jessica became angry and said, "I want to go to Hale [another school in the city] because they have a better OLC program." Mr. Maddy began to gather up his papers. He told her, "Perhaps you are venting your hostility now, saying that Hale has a better program." Using the language of the students, he said, "Are you playing me, Jessica?" Jessica said, "I want what I want." At this point, the loud-speaker went on again, announcing that several teachers had not delivered their attendance sheets to the main office and that they should bring them immediately.

After the announcement, Jessica repeated herself again, saying that she could not enter the OLC program because she worked. Supporting Jessica for the first time, the caseworker asked, "Couldn't she go into the day school?" Mr. Maddy shook his head and asked, "What about care for the baby?" Jessica said, "I told you. I'm working on that." Mr. Maddy then brought up the GED program, which is also during the afternoon school. He said that most of the work was done through packets, and though they hoped that students would come to the classes, they could, in fact, do most of the program on their own, at their own speed, and not attend the preparation classes. Jessica did not want the GED program. It was quite obvious that she wanted to be reinstated in day school. Ms. Evers then said, "You can try the ELDP." "When's that?" Jessica asked, and Ms. Evers told her, "In afternoon school." Again, Jessica said, "I work in the afternoon! What about the day?"

For the next 5 minutes, Mr. Maddy explained to Jessica that she could not enter day school. He ticked off the reasons: She would not be able to adapt to the schedule; she already had past problems with attendance; day school started at 8:00. He said, "Five days a week, each day, and you are expected to be here. Can you handle that? I don't think so." Larry Ryan, who had been silent, said, "I think Mr. M. is right." Jessica became silent again, returning her gaze to the tabletop.

Finally, Mr. Maddy asked Jessica, "What do you want? What program do you want?" Jessica said, "Regular school." Mr. Maddy asked her, "Are you sure? In spite of the early days?" Jessica nodded. It seemed that Jessica was about to get her way when Mr. Ryan said, "I believe Mr. M. is correct.

If we put you in day school we will be setting you up for failure." Jessica pulled the hood of her parka almost entirely over her face, completely defeated now. She looked at the clock and said, "I have to go." Mr. Maddy said to the caseworker, "Talk to her. Take her down to the Johnson Center and see what programs they have open. In the meantime, we'll see about the afternoon program here."

Jessica got up and left the room. The caseworker lagged behind and told us that she would see what she could do. Mr. Maddy told the caseworker, "She's a tough one," and the caseworker nodded. Once the caseworker had left, Mr. Maddy remarked to the group, "She works at night and has to take a bus from the north side. What's the chances of her being victimized?" He seemed disgusted. "Who would let their daughters do that?" he said. I said, "She'd been kicked out of her house," and he responded, "She still has a mother." Mr. Maddy turned to the group and said, "She's 16, has a child, no education, and on top of that, I would say an identity problem. She talks black English." Ms. Evers remarked, in a knowing way, "I'm sure her boyfriend is black."

A variety of issues and factors converged in the meeting with Jessica, most of them things that hurt her but were beyond her control. Take, for example, the stress that the staff were already feeling because of the suicide threat and the anxiety that was caused by the bomb threats that were regularly being called into the school at the time. Jessica was a kid who had already been abandoned by her family, and was about to be abandoned by the school. In addition, she was shy, and discouraged from expressing herself (except to repeat her desire to be in day school) by personal questions and a blaring PA system. She caused people to be angry by doing the right thing—wanting to get to work on time. Like Jamil, she did not know how, or refused, to act in a cordial, slightly subservient, and respectful way.

Jessica was not known personally; rather, her type was known. In the minds of school staff—who could get to know her only in terms of her hostile actions and bad habits—she was the quintessential abandoned white girl, making her way on the streets, living off of both white and black men, and ready to be victimized by them. She had a baby, and though she told the committee that she had had a difficult pregnancy that kept her out of school—which was true of many girls in this city where infant mortality is among the highest in the nation—the committee would not talk to her about what she wanted. Reeling from their own stresses, the committee members wore Jessica down and, as in Jamil's case, got her guardian (in this instance, a caseworker) to side with them—all of which was done as if it were for Jessica's own good. After all, the assistant principal (who had arrived late and really did not know what was going on or who the girl was) pointed out that we do not want to be "setting up students for failure."

But not all screening committee meetings were battles between students and staff. In the next case, Renail, who was black, arrived with a baby, a happy attitude, and a willingness to do what the committee said was best. Perhaps one of every three or four meetings went smoothly like this. Renail's vignette is but one example of how this happens.

CASE III
It was a cool, clear afternoon, the first sunny day in weeks, it seemed. Renail was the third student to come before the screening committee. She was 17 years old and African American. As usual, the screening committee sat chatting around the table waiting for a student to arrive. Ms. Evers, looking over Renail's school file, noted that "she was dropped" last year because of absenteeism.

Renail came in, swinging at her hip a carrier with a 4-month-old baby. She arrived with her caseworker, as well, an older African American woman who helped carry a bag of diapers and baby toys. Renail, who seemed cheerful, placed her baby in the carrier on the table and Ms. Evers, Mr. Maddy, and a teacher from the special education program all leaned forward and peeked at the baby. Mr. Maddy remarked about the baby's cuteness. Renail took off her coat, sat, and gently rocked the baby carrier. The baby was fast asleep. The caseworker kept her coat and hat on and also sat.

After Mr. Maddy introduced the committee, Ms. Evers remarked about Ranail's attendance record and Renail said, "I missed so much here and at Y Med." Y Med was a city school for pregnant girls and new young mothers. Renail explained, nodding at her baby, "This one was 3 months too soon." The caseworker showed the group the palm of her hand and said, "She was no bigger than this." Renail explained that she had been going to Y Med but had discontinued because she had had a difficult pregnancy. Ms. Evers nodded and asked Renail, "What are you interested in?" Renail thought for a moment, then said, "I don't know." The caseworker explained that any decision that was made must take into account the baby. "The baby was born premature and has special needs," she said. Mr. Maddy asked Renail if she had child care, and Renail told him that she was working on it, but that it was very difficult to find the right person because the baby had a lot of needs.

Mr. Maddy asked, "Whom do you live with?" Renail said, "With the baby's father." The caseworker added, "Also with the father's mother. So there is an adult presence in the house." Renail nodded. Mr. Maddy seemed content with this answer. He explained the GED program in the afternoon school and told her that it was primarily "packet driven." He explained that students could work at their own pace, that the program met in the afternoon, and that there was not a mandatory attendance policy. "This might be a good program for you, with the baby, your needs." He told her she could come to the program "anywhere from 3 to 5 days a week. There's a lot of seat work involved."

Renail seemed to think for a moment. She asked, "How long do I got to attend?" Mr. Maddy told her that she could take the test any time. "But you have to be prepared for it. It costs money. Fifty bucks a pop." Renail nodded. "That's expensive," she said. Mr. Maddy told her, "It's not an easy test. There is a lot of seat work and time-on-task preparation work you'll have to do. But this will prepare you for the test, because it's 6 hours long, and that's a long time. Most students are not used to sitting that long." Ms. Evers also mentioned that there was a job developer who came to Brandon High during the afternoon school program. "He can help you find a job." Renail's baby made a sputtering sound and Renail gave the carrier a little rock. Mr. Maddy asked her if she had a job and Renail told him that she worked at Burger King. "You really should see the job developer," he said. "You could get a better job maybe." Mr. Ryan, who had been quiet during the session, asked if she had transportation and she told him that she could take the bus.

The meeting seemed to end on a positive note for everybody. The committee agreed that Renail would enter the GED program after the winter holiday. She would stay in the program until she decided to take the GED test and passed it, and she would contact the job developer to check out possibilities for a better job. Renail seemed pleased with all this. She and the caseworker thanked the committee and left.

The entire mood of this meeting was different from many others, but was typical of those that went smoothly. Renail was being helped by a caring guardian and the wants of the school did not deviate from those of Renail and her guardian. Renail lived with the father of her child, both were presumably of the same race, she had a job, and seemed to want to do right by her daughter. On top of this, the sun was out in a city that was often gloomy and people's moods were optimistic. These were circumstances that pleased the screening committee, so Renail was promptly registered for afternoon school without fuss.

Meanwhile, she had had a difficult pregnancy that derailed her schooling, she worked at Burger King at minimum wage, and she was doing her best to be a good mother and to do what was best for her own education. Her circumstances show how one mishap leads to another, how stressors pile up one on top of the other—from a difficult pregnancy, to a baby with more needs than most, and then the difficultly of finding a daycare provider for such a baby. At the very least, Renail should be guaranteed a stellar education and living wage so that her ambitions can be fulfilled in spite of these overwhelming circumstances.

In spite of the apparent optimism of everybody involved in this meeting, the fact remains that after Renail's difficult pregnancy prevented her from attending school, she was "dropped" from the roll. Given the school's limitations, its tracking system, its busy and stressed staff, and the severe problems of many students, perhaps a quarter of the students were left to the devices of a system that steered them into the subtracks of the school and then into a city that offered them little help or support, and few chances for stable employment with a salary they could live on. These students needed something more, something better. Some of these students managed to pull themselves through, though. People like Renail who had a professional disposition, family support, and sheer will and smarts could pull through. College, well-paying jobs, security, and happiness were still feasible. But this was not the case for many students, such as Avery, whose bouts with the law, poor health, and problems with learning in school had already put him on the prison track.

CASE IV

Avery, an ex-Brandon High student, arrived at his screening committee meeting with an electronic security bracelet around his ankle. School staff referred to these as "electronic leashes." The bracelet was mandated by the city court as an alternative to incarceration; it tracked Avery's whereabouts and could be taken off only by his parole officer. Avery was 17 years old and African American. He arrived with his mother and his great-grandfather. At the time of his screening, he was under house arrest.

Before the meeting, the principal, who had decided to sit in with the committee, told me that the mother was very religious, and that Avery had gone to "bible camp" last summer instead of the required summer school program. In addition, during the summer, Avery had been arrested for trying to run somebody over with his mother's car. While the circumstances of the incident were unclear, an assistant principal who happened to be in the room getting coffee at the time remarked about the case. He said that in court Avery's family had tried to convince the judge that Avery had been acting in self-defense—essentially, responding to boys who had been threatening him. Ms. Evers explained that it was another "simple, plain, gang case."

"It doesn't matter," Ms. Street said, closing the door to the conference room. "Remember, we want to get an address," she said. "Let's play the custody card." Ms. Evers looked at some paperwork and noted that Ave. had proof that he lived in the school district. Ms. Street turned to Mr. Maddy: "We'll have to take him, then." She told the group not to mention special education or "LD" (learning disabled) programs. She said, "If they bring it up, we'll take it from there and work with it, but let's not mention it if we don't have to." Avery had been diagnosed with a learning disability but Brandon High did not offer special education in afternoon school and therefore according to law could not place him there.

Avery came in with his family. After Mr. Maddy introduced the group, he sat between his mother and great-grandfather. Avery, who was very tall, towered over his mother, who was formally dressed and smelled of perfume. She promptly began to explain the situation; she wanted to get right to business. She explained that Avery was under house arrest, that his movements were restricted, and that he had already been in prison and had just been released the day before. Referring to the charge, the mother said that it was a self-defense case, but the court did not recognize this. Avery's great-grandfather agreed. He sat with his hands folded in his lap and remarked, "America does not have any respect for self-defense." Avery's mother explained that Avery had also been in foster care. She said, "God is good, though, and has taken care of Avery. I do believe my Avery will put himself together." During the meeting, the mother seemed to introduce each of her statements with the phrases "God is good" or "We are a Christian family."

Mr. Maddy asked Avery if he worked. Avery looked at Mr. Maddy and said, "What?" Mr. Maddy repeated the question. Avery nodded slowly. First, he said that he did work, but when Mr. Maddy asked him where he worked, he said, "Actually, I don't work," but he did not seem to be trying to lie. Rather, he seemed confused. Mr. Maddy suggested that he get into Central Tech, but his mother did not want that. She said, "We are a Christian family and that's where the troublemakers are. The people Avery has to stay away from. I want him in school. That's where he belongs. I want him in classes." The principal had already told the group that she did not want Avery in day school.

Mr. Maddy explained that if he were to reenter the OLC program—where he was before his arrest—he would have to go to Central Tech. "There's the occupational learning component to the OLC program," he explained. "Avery can learn welding." The mother wanted day school and insisted that Avery did not belong in afternoon school. Ms. Street stiffened. Mr. Maddy asked Ms. Evers how many credits Avery had and Ms. Evers said, "Six that I can see." Mr. Maddy explained to the mother, "That means that he has just finished the ninth grade. At 17, he's old enough to be a senior." The mother explained that he was 2 years behind because he was

t, Mr. Maddy explained that the GED program might
old her that there were other boys under house arrest
and that the school was in close contact with all the
. When Avery's ready to take the GED test, he could have
to help him with understanding the questions since he's dyslexic.
..at we can do."

The great-grandfather mentioned that he had gotten his GED and had done fine in life. "Worked over 30 years in the factory. Got my GED." The mother would not hear of it. She insisted that Avery be let back into the regular day school. She was not angry, but she was insistent and very artic-ulate. "I believe Avery deserves day school. That is where he belongs. God is good, and will take care of my Avery." Mr. Ryan, who had been listening intently, said to Avery, "Do you remember your old buddy, Terry York? He's in the OLC program, and doing well." Then, half talking to the mother, he said, "Terry's mother didn't want him going to the day school because she was afraid for his safety." This seemed to strike a nerve in Avery's mother. She stiffened, then nodded. Quietly, she said, "We worry about that too." Mr. Ryan explained that there was better security in the afternoon program, better supervision, and fewer students. "It's safer for kids who have had brushes with gangs." Avery's mother snapped, "My boy ain't no gang banger." Mr. Ryan, not wanting to argue, conceded: "I know, I know," he said.

The mother mentioned that her son had very bad asthma and therefore needed a nurse. Mr. Maddy said that there was a nurse on call during afternoon school. The mother mentioned that Avery was also in foster care. "God is good, and takes care of Avery," she said. Mr. Ryan assured her that this was okay. "There's a lot of kids with alternative family arrangements," he said. Avery's mother began to give in and asked about the GED program. In the end, it was determined that Avery would go into the GED program. "It's the faster route for students to get their equivalency diploma," Mr. Ryan explained. Mr. Maddy explained that some students do very well with a GED degree. He mentioned that some go on to community colleges, then transfer to liberal arts colleges.

After the meeting, Mr. Maddy remarked about Avery's mother: "She sure has a warped sense of attempted murder—it's not knowing what you are doing mixed with a bit of self-defense!" He mentioned that he had had Avery in his special education classes for 2 years. The principal joked, "It's successes like that that keep us going."

A student like Avery in a regular high school like Brandon High does not succeed. Besides his family and perhaps himself, nobody actually be-lieves that he is capable of succeeding. There was nothing in Brandon High to help him succeed, and Avery's mother seemed to know this. She fought half-heartedly for Avery's admittance to day school but was worldly enough to know that even if admitted he would not last there. She was talking to people who did not want Avery and she knew this. She fought harder for his respect—growing angriest when defending her son ("my boy ain't no gang banger"). She wanted the group to know about his problems, to try to understand him in the way she knew him.

Ultimately, though, Avery's mother put more stock in a miracle from God than in the school. The screening committee, bending the law and covering up truths about the services in afternoon school, operated with the knowledge that there was not an official—not in the school, not in the downtown central office—who wanted kids like Avery in school. Too much money, too many efforts and facilities have already gone into the alternative school placements and the creation of afternoon schools (in all of the high schools in the city) to have Avery in regular school. He was a kid caught up in gangs; he was being victimized and was violent against others; he had been in prison; he was large, black; he did not learn as fast as others; he had medical problems; he was dyslexic; and in the minds of business-oriented school administrators, he would be expensive to educate.

At 17 years of age, with only six credits, Avery had run out of time. The only option now was afternoon school, which school staff made appealing by associating it with the protection it could offer the boy. The mother was ultimately swayed when the assistant principal made use of her fear about Avery's safety to secure the boy's placement in the GED program. If Avery ever sits next to Renail in the GED program classroom, though, it won't be for long. For Avery, GED was a ticket out of school, and everybody knew this, including Avery and his mother. It was doubtful he would even register. At the end of the meeting the talk about college for Avery was fake, and the last statement by the principal held an ironic truth about what were considered "successes" by a school.

ON PLACING AND DROPPING STUDENTS

The work that the screening committee did at Brandon High can be viewed from different perspectives. In one way, the committee reproduced in students' school lives the alienation they were already experiencing outside of school (see Bogdan & Taylor, 1994). As a gateway into the afternoon school program it relegated students to nonacademic programs and ultimately inferior credentials on graduation from high school—if they do graduate. For kids like Avery, the committee produced a self-fulfilling prophecy: Students are deemed deviant, they are treated as deviants, and therefore deviate as is expected of them (see Becker, 1963; Goffman, 1963; Rist, 1970). The screening committee was part of a larger organization of "alternative placements" that channeled some students to lives that at best would entail menial labor (welding, "nails") and at worst prison or violent death—a kind of sorting machine (Apple, 1978; Bowles & Gintis, 1976; Giroux, 1983). Jessica, Jamil, and most other students, and many parents, knew that the committee's decisions were not always in the best interest of students, though they may have been in the best interest of a school concerned about control, safety, and its reputation in the city. While the afternoon school provided some students who could not attend day school an alternative to dropping out, it was also a tracking system for losers. In the tracked school system, afternoon school was below the lowest track of the regular day school.

Even students who had babies, such as Jessica, and who may have feared for their safety, such as Jamil and Avery, sometimes wished to enter day school in spite of their worries and hardships. They recognized the second-class status of students placed in afternoon school and seemed to feel that at worst they would end up dropping or failing out of day school, but to them it was worth the risk. In fact, Mr. Ryan was right to say that a placement in day school would be "setting students up for failure." Most of these students would probably not succeed in day school for the simple reason that day school was not set up for them. It would not meet their needs and did not have what it took to work with them; unfortunately neither did the afternoon school.

But not all students in afternoon school were unhappy being there. Some actually preferred it. Two students in a discussion in the hallway after day school told me that they felt safer in afternoon school. One told me, "The time you want to be in school is during the afternoon when all the trouble in the neighborhoods starts." He was absolutely right too; crime rose in the area between 3:00 and 6:00 in the evening as school let out. Others who seemed to lack motivation or did not wish to meet the challenge of schooling claimed that afternoon school was easier and therefore preferred their stays there. Some students had jobs during the day or needed to care for children, which made the possibility of day school unlikely.

While some students went to afternoon school reluctantly, the screening committee was not an unobstructed entryway into afternoon school. There were times when the screening committee would not send a student to afternoon school. In one case a girl who arrived for screening and requested afternoon school was 14 years old. The student had been at another public school in the city, was on PINS (Persons In Need of Supervision), and at the time was living with cousins. The committee recommended that the student enter the day school 9-A team. This was a group of about 12 students who were in the ninth grade but moved together with a teacher to each of their classes. They had been deemed too young for the afternoon school but too far behind in their class work to take regular classes. Students in the 9-A team ended up in either regular 10th-grade classes or in the afternoon school program. There was not a 10-A team.

It was rare that students in screening committee meetings actually wanted to be in afternoon school. And yet, in spite of students' protests, and in some cases the advocacy of parents, students were not often allowed back into day school. White girls such as Jessica, who had urban accents and boyfriends who may have been black, were sometimes deemed incapable because of moral deficiencies. Committee meeting talk revolved around babies, boyfriends, how the girls got home at night, and how late they slept in the mornings. These were issues that rarely surfaced with boys or with black girls. White girls were thought of not only as academically incapable but also as lacking in the values and habits conducive to being good female students—the social upbringing, the conformity, the avoidance of miscegenation. They were an embarrassment.

On the other hand, students like Renail—who were either pregnant or had a baby, and black—were the easiest because they rarely requested day school. Many of the African American girls I met wanted to tend to their babies, and sometimes had to do so full time when fathers were not present. I did not know if Renail was religious but in other committee meetings girls from religious African American families were sometimes persuaded by family members that they must give up day school. When they did request day school, they, like other students, were often persuaded that afternoon school was appropriate, and most importantly, in their and their babies' best interests. This was always the point of screening committee meetings: to convince students that their placements, whatever they might be, were not only appropriate but also best suited for them. The quicker a student accepted this, the easier the screening committee meeting went.

The African American boys often came to the table with experiences involving gangs, failure in school, lack of support, and brushes (and sometimes hard time) with the criminal justice system. These students were promptly steered to afternoon school or to other schools in the city, such as the Alternative School or to JVC for adult education classes. Often screening committee members saw no hope in their lives and expected not much more than prison in their futures. Though they may have protested, as Jamil did, their expectations were low, for they seemed all too well acquainted with a public system that offered no hope to the young, the black, and the delinquent. They did not protest for long. They either found a niche in afternoon school, a group to be down with, or they dropped out. In knowing ways they conceded to the wishes of the school as they had to juvenile courts, foster homes, and other public services.

Though none of the vignettes deal with white boys, when these cases did come up—which was rare—committee discussions usually revolved around the importance of hard work and the students' futures as laborers in the trades. Of the 30 or so students that I saw in screening committee meetings, four of them were white boys. One lived outside the district and was quickly dismissed by the committee; the other three were steered to vocational education. In each case the committee emphasized to these working-class guys the importance of learning a trade and the benefits of the OLC program. And in each of the three cases the students agreed that OLC would suffice—that it would enable them to enter Central Tech and get a job.

Issues of race, disability, gender, and class entered into decisions about students' placements but they did not determine placements. Equally influential was the reputation of the student or the student's history. Reflecting the school's primary concern, which was violence, students who had been extremely violent in the past—regardless of who they were—were often steered out of school entirely. The white boy who did not live in the district and was dismissed by the committee was also a student who had been extremely violent in the past. Eric was 17 years old, and arrived with both of his parents. The year before he had assaulted two female students from Brandon High and was considered, as the principal noted, "very bad news." His assaults on the students had been reported in the city newspaper. In the meeting I attended the committee would not let Eric back in school, and used the central office to prove that he lived outside the district. Although Eric was living with his grandmother in the Brandon High School district, his mother, who lived outside the district, had custody of him. Ultimately, Mr. Maddy pointed out to Eric's parents that Eric did not live in the district and that Brandon High would not accept him—case closed.

The cases not only highlight how screening committee decisions were made but also the challenges that the committee faced in dealing with students whose lives were in ruins. These were students who were in the words of some school staff on the "prison track" or at a "dead end" in their lives. Many of the boys, especially the black students, had been in boot camps or prisons—as was the case with Avery and Eric. Jamil seemed emotionally traumatized by the loss of his twin sister. Some of the students, white and African American, had zero credits at age 18. At a time when they should have been graduating, they had in fact never successfully completed a single high school class. Other students had been knifed, shot, or hospitalized, and had missed a lot of school. Many of the students had difficulty proving their addresses or stating who their guardians were. Some students—es-

pecially girls—were runaways, some escaping abusiv
students arrived with caseworkers, sometimes with o
times, students owed money to lawyers, which had c
she had to work and therefore could not attend day s
unjust treatment of students by committee member;
this explosive context: It is not only schools that are ᵣₐᵢₗᵢₙᵧ
but also families and communities. And since this is a problem that devas-
tates many cities, not just Brandon city, the fault lies not only with communities but also with the policies and actions of a nation that has produced
such dire circumstances for city youth.

SUSPENSION AND EXPULSION

As depressing as these stories are, nothing is more disheartening than the
fact that for decades influential and clear-thinking individuals have criticized the kinds of school behavior that push students out through suspension, expulsion, and afternoon school programs. Yet little is done to assure
that troubled students like Jessica, Jamil, and others stay in school produc-
tively. As noted earlier, in the 1970s, the U.S. Congress commissioned a
study of school violence and vandalism by the Department of Health, Education, and Welfare, which resulted in the *Safe School Study* (NIE, 1977).
In addition to the actual National Institute of Education report to Congress, the Congress's own internal Subcommittee to Investigate Juvenile
Delinquency held two hearings. The subcommittee was led by Senator
Birch Bayh of Indiana, who released a preliminary report entitled *Our Nation's Schools—A Report Card: "A" in School Violence and Vandalism.*

During the hearings, Bayh argued a point that should be understood
by now by all screening committees: that suspension and expulsion are
meted out to students unjustly and cause students to feel frustrated and
perhaps violent.

> It has been brought to the attention of the committee . . . that part of the
> problem with violence and vandalism is that the discipline level is not adminis-
> tered equitably and equally across the board; that students are sometimes ex-
> pelled without any explanation. Teachers and school administrators are not
> perfect. They get a story that might be a wrong story and could be explained.
> . . . And, if the student is not given a bill of particulars, the reaction might be
> violence—particularly in the student area where there are racial minorities
> involved, where a child is very uptight because of prejudice. Although he or
> she might have committed a grievance that required discipline, if that disci-
> pline is not explained to him in detail, it might reawaken all the old prejudices
> to which they have been subjected. (in Toby, 1994, p. 41)

Senator Bayh reiterated a position that was expressed by Marian Wright Edelman during the second round of hearings. She explained that "the solution to school violence does not lie in more suspensions but less, for its causes are to be found more on the streets where dropouts, pushouts, and suspended students pass the time" (quoted in Toby, 1994, p. 42). Both Edelman and Bayh were critical of the practices, and while stopping short of disallowing them, they called for greater care and documentation of expulsions and suspensions. In some ways, they were repeating federal laws that already required that schools provide students due process in suspension and expulsion cases, which would include written explanations of the charges against them.

Part of what drives the screening committee is the requirement to abide by due process policy: The screening committee is actually set up to protect kids. The U.S. Supreme Court ruling in *Goss v. Lopez* (1975) stated that students were entitled to due process when threatened with either suspension or expulsion. The Supreme Court required that schools provide a written notice and a judicial hearing—hence, screening committee—as part of the process in order to avoid unfair or mistaken exclusion from the educational process. In this case, the Court wrote:

> The concern would be mostly academic if the disciplinary process were a totally accurate, unerring process, never mistaken and never unfair. Unfortunately, that is not the case, and no one suggests that it is. Disciplinarians, although proceeding in utmost good faith, frequently act on the reports and advice of others; and the . . . facts and the nature of the conduct under challenge are often disputed. The risk of error is not at all trivial, and it should be guarded against if that may be done without prohibitive cost or interference with the educational process. (quoted in Lawrence, 1998, p. 148)

As a result of the hearing by the Subcommittee to Investigate Juvenile Delinquency and the *Goss v. Lopez* ruling, schools have devised elaborate procedures for the suspension and expulsion of students. Unfortunately, the procedures make the process more bureaucratic rather than more fair.

At Brandon High, students had to be given oral and written explanations of their alleged crimes; their guardians had to be notified; central office had to be given a written explanation of the charges; and in many cases students had to stand before a Superintendent's Hearing. This was all part of due process. But with so many students being suspended and expelled, and entering and exiting the school through the screening committee, due process became streamlined into forms to be signed and placements to be sealed. The screening committee was a part of this process, as were the assistant principals' offices and the secretaries, all of whom churned out incredible amounts of paperwork to officiate and legitimize the job.

Certainly some of the students who went before the screening committee at Brandon High were messed up, but messed up did not necessarily mean violent—and certainly not violent in all circumstances. Take away the gangs, the community breakdown, the everyday abuses, the institutional blocks, the systemic violence, and these were students who could quite possibly pull it together. Instead, the naturalness of the established punitive order, the acceptance of zero tolerance, and the circumstances that drove students to criminal and self-destructive behavior in the first place persist to create a school system that lacks caring and students who in the end give up on themselves and simply take what is coming to them.

THE "IN" OF OUTPLACEMENTS

In general, policy that has legitimized greater use of suspension, expulsion, and various forms of outplacement has undermined the education of students who, though difficult and even violent, need guidance, help, and an institution that can work *with* them. In these cases, students are not only treated poorly by a school system, but they also take part in the process by ultimately accepting their placements and by continuing the violent activities that put them in such positions. Willis (1977) and Bourdieu (1991) explained that the power of a school to steer students to particular placements can be exercised only with the complicity of the students themselves. But students at Brandon High did not go quietly. Unfortunately, their fights (and those of their guardians) dwindled without the knowledge and power to influence the decisions that were made.

By law, the screening committee could not deny youth access to day school unless the students did not have residency in the district. At the same time, the school had real worries about violence and public perceptions that would label their building violent—which could lead to other serious problems, including a greater exodus of families and students from the school. The students who went before the screening committee were not completely abandoned by the school system, since law does not permit this. They were segregated within the system—not "outplaced" but "inplaced." Their futures were determined by individuals who foremost desired a safe and disciplined school, who knew they could not completely turn students away but who were able to find out-of-the-way niches for them. Students accepted their placements in spite of momentary and sometimes energized protests. Once in afternoon school, students seemed to hang out just fine if they came at all—protests for the most part ended after the initial sound and fury in screening committee meetings.

While the law protected some students, the development in recent years of afternoon schools, Homebound Instruction, and other such "alternative" placements has led to greater ineffectiveness of compulsory education laws and the incapability of students to press their cases to stay in day school. It remains correct today as it did in earlier decades that "excluding the more unruly from school would be excluding those students who are not now helped to perform well in school" (Gottfredson & Gottfredson, 1985, p. 191). Being in-placed means that students are still considered in school by the central office and by law, but that they are receiving an education significantly inferior to that of day school. In addition, more punitive juvenile delinquent, status offender, and drug laws have led to greater numbers of black males in prison, which undermines equal educational opportunity if not compulsory education laws. The result has been more education programs in prisons, not more students in day school.

Partly an outcome of Education Law 3214, which states that when a student of compulsory school age is suspended or expelled a school district must provide alternative instruction, the screening committee acts as an entryway into the city's maze of in- and outplacements. Schools such as Brandon High are following laws (but not always), as well as state guidelines and school policies. But they are also responding to rhetoric of violence and youth that has called for the abandonment of students like Avery, as well as Eddie Barron, whose story is discussed in the next chapter. The rhetoric and the facilities that have been set up to monitor these students have legitimized by consensus the prosecution of young people who have been as much victims of violence as perpetrators of it. No doubt there were students in Brandon High, people like Eric and maybe Avery, who were real trouble. These were not innocent victims. They took abuse and they gave it out. But schools have an obligation to help these students—or at least to try.

The impersonal quality that some claim is characteristic of bureaucracies is bit of an overstatement. These students did not move through the maze of in- and outplacements as faceless entities. They were well known to school staff, and because of this there seemed to be little reason for the committee to try to learn anything new from them about what might help them. They were written off. They were "dropped" as far down the social hierarchy as one could go. Being down for them was more than a state of mind, it was their place in a carefully crafted institutional niche set up for the young, the poor, and the delinquent. Decades ago these kids might have found work in the city factories of which Avery's grandfather spoke. Today, with more squatters than workers in the factories, they feed the ever-expanding prison system.

CHAPTER 4

Of Hood Rats and City Cops

The screening committee, along with afternoon school, was a way of keeping track of students. As one assistant principal remarked: "We have over
1,300 students in school—in afternoon school it's much less, so we can
keep an eye on them." Once students were placed in one of the afternoon
programs, the school police officer was notified and then charged with the
task of watching over students. The police officer's job, then, was to make
his presence known to the new afternoon school students by continually
being visible. He met late incoming students at the door, meandered
through the halls, and finally went home at 6:00 after seeing the last of
these students leave. When necessary he was the link among the afternoon
school program, the screening committee, and the city police department.

In one case, for example, a student who had a warrant out for his
arrest came before the screening committee. Eddie Barron had been expelled from Brandon High the year before after stabbing a girl in the hand
with a pencil. In addition, during the winter vacation in December, he and
another student from Brandon High were at the city mall where they
stabbed a rival gang member in the buttocks. During the struggle a police
officer was almost thrown or he almost fell (the stories were mixed) over
the second-story railing of the mall atrium.

When Detective O'Hara saw Eddie come into the school for his screening, he went to his office to call the police department to verify the warrant.
In addition to the pencil stabbing and the knife fight, Eddie's warrant included assault and possession of a weapon. An assistant principal came
into the office and O'Hara put his hand over the receiver of the phone and
told him, "We might have to 12 him" (meaning arrest him). The assistant
principal requested that the police department send a marked car and
O'Hara relayed the message into the phone. He then unlocked his desk
drawer and took out and shook pepper spray and clipped handcuffs to the
holster of his gun. The assistant principal left to get the principal. A few
minutes later, Detective O'Hara and the principal talked over the situation
and the principal pressed O'Hara not to arrest Eddie right away since his
father was with him.

I joined the screening committee as Eddie and his father came into the room. Detective O'Hara waited just outside the door. Eddie sat on one side of the table and kept his jacket on. He seemed to be somewhat tired and not very attentive. At one point, the principal asked him, "Did you get enough sleep last night?" but Eddie did not answer. After the meeting, Mr. Maddy remarked that Eddie was always like that—"half in a daze"— and the principal suggested that he was stoned. Ms. Evers agreed. Mr. Maddy said, "Sure, he's always stoned," and Ms. Street said, "But he seemed more stoned that usual." Given that students are increasingly prescribed drugs, however, he could also have been under the influence of medication such as methylphenidate or its derivative, Ritalin.

Eddie was 17 years old and wanted to enter the Occupational Learning Center (OLC) program. He had just been released from prison and had been on Homebound Instruction for 6 months. Ms. Evers looked at Eddie's paperwork and remarked that he only had two school credits, which he earned during summer school. Eddie was living with his father but his father, a large man in a biker jacket, seemed fed up with him. At one point the father said to the committee, "He's wasting your time. You should just kick him out." Eddie showed no reaction when his father said this. Mr. Maddy told Eddie that he could get his GED and graduate in June if he worked hard. Eddie said that he did not want to graduate in June. "What do I do *then*?" he asked. After the meeting, Mr. Maddy referred to this statement—Eddie's apparent reluctance to graduate—by saying, "Eddie knows that as soon as he graduates there is nothing between him and the prison system. The school couldn't save him anymore."

Mr. Maddy told Eddie that he could go to Central Tech without enrolling in the OLC program. He could get his GED, then learn welding. Eddie said that he did not want to learn welding and for a moment his father seemed to support him: "He'll end up going blind doing welding." Eddie kept saying that he did not want to go down to Central Tech by himself, without being in the OLC program. The last time he went to check there were no openings. At this point the assistant principal intervened, ignoring the point the boy had made. He told Eddie that the Central Tech program was unique. He explained that most of the teachers were not really educators but people who used to be in the working trades. Offering Eddie a warning, he said, "These are not people who are very concerned about student self-esteem, they are straight-ahead people, like in the army. They don't put up with meatheads. If you try to give them an attitude, they will take care of you very quickly."

The committee went back and forth with Eddie, trying to convince him to get his GED and to enter a Central Tech program. Eddie remained reluctant. In the end, his father threw up his hands and yelled at Eddie,

"Will you stop wasting these people's time!" He rose from his chair and told Eddie to follow him. They left the room. Nothing had been agreed on, which did not matter since it had already been determined that Eddie would be arrested.

Police departments pick up the slack when schools fail. According to 19th-century plans, officers were never meant to appear in school buildings, but police officers have not only appeared; they have become integral parts of school systems. They make distinctions between the school and the city police department nearly disappear—blurred by faxes and telephone calls between the school and the police station, the standard police cruiser in the school parking lot, and computer data provided by city police researchers but used by the school. In many discussions throughout the school year, Detective O'Hara made it clear to me that he was, in his words, "first a police officer and second a school worker," but the reality of his days was not so distinct.

In what follows, I step out of the school building to examine policing in Brandon city, before turning specifically to school policing in the next chapter. This is a way of viewing school violence within the context of the city but also of understanding what Detective O'Hara means when he says "first a police officer." Regardless of one's position on school policing and the euphemisms one uses to designate their jobs ("school safety officers," "juvenile aid workers," etc.), the school officer is essentially a *police officer*. If we are to understand the nature of school policing, which is perhaps the most dramatic change that schools have undergone in recent years as a response to violence, we must first understand the nature and role of policing in urban areas (what is meant by "being a police officer"). This chapter focuses on two interrelated themes that emerged in conversations, interviews, and observations of police: the isolation that Brandon city police officers felt from the community and the court system, and the strained relationships that existed between officers and Brandon city residents, especially those who were poor and black.

ENTER THE POLICE

Discussions about urban police have often revolved around themes associated with police culture, norms, training, and bureaucratic structures (Neiderhoffer, 1967; Terry, 1985; Yarmey, 1990). In recent years greater emphasis has been placed on "subcultural" considerations that are meant to explain how police officers come to view themselves as a distinct group and sometimes in opposition to the general public (Weitzer & Tuch, 1999). While some of this more recent work focuses on the negative aspects of law enforcement, evoked in book titles such as *Forces of Deviance: Understanding the Dark Side of Policing* (Kappeler, Sluder, & Alpert, 1994), criticism of urban police is not new. Turn-of-the-century Progressives, who wanted to counteract growing city machines, attacked police departments because of their involvement in city patronage. Their work paralleled that of muckrakers who exposed police corruption and graft in pointed articles for select magazines. George Turner wrote in 1907 in *McClure's*, the famous muckraking magazine: "The addition of the police force completes the great organization for the exploitation of savagery. . . . The dealer in dissipation, the ward boss and the police official are its chief members" (quoted in Weinberg & Weinberg, 1964, p. 403). Along with Progressive reformers and muckrakers, individuals in the emerging profession of social work also criticized police for their favored strong-arm tactics against new immigrants and their neglecting enforcement of vice laws in protected neighborhoods (Feld, 1999).

But interspersed in the history of police corruption are examples of police benevolence and community involvement. As Kelling and Coles (1998, p. 242) noted, since the 19th century police have had a long history of providing services for urban communities. Original police stations were built with extra space to house new migrants who moved to the city from rural areas. Officers were trained to help homeless people contact social service agencies and the original food and soup lines were developed by police forces. Certainly some police departments were and remain corrupt and sometimes brutal, but police organizations are neither completely benevolent nor completely crooked. Police develop animosities toward the public at the same time that they adhere to a belief system that helps them to view themselves, in the words of one Brandon city police officer, as "good guys in a sea of bad."

Though I conducted formal interviews with police officers and shadowed some on their beats (something that any Brandon city resident can do as part of the police department's "community policing" attempt to improve relations with city residents), most of my interviews were informal. They occurred in the hallway at the police station, in Brandon High when city police were there, at community meetings, and even on the street. In these informal situations, discussions with police often led to conversations about their role. Many seemed anxious to explain that their role was limited, that they "could only do so much," and that they were only one part of a larger system.

One Brandon city police officer spoke for many when he explained his job: "My work is to take care of the business at hand. I get the criminals in cuffs, take them downtown, get the paperwork in, and send 'em off to the district attorneys' office. They pick it up from there." Even in this brief description, he hinted at his role in a larger system and his distance from the people he served. Like cogs in a vast system of machinery, some do their impersonal parts and move on. This is what the Bureau of Justice Assistance (1994) referred to as "social distancing"—the way police and residents create rifts that separate them. To counteract social distancing, one policy reaction in recent years has been the development of community policing initiatives, which Marans and Schaefer (1998, p. 323) summarized as efforts to

1. Develop mutual trust and community partnerships that define mutually agreed on priorities.
2. Exceed law enforcement in recognizing the value of activities that contribute to the orderliness and well-being of the community and its members (e.g., helping crime victims, resolving family and community disputes, making referrals for those at risk, and providing models of positive/good citizenship).
3. Accord respect and sensitivity to all citizens in an evenhanded, just fashion.
4. Use in-depth knowledge of neighborhoods as the basis for understanding root causes of difficulties and engaging in problem solving.
5. Use law enforcement agencies as catalysts for mobilizing resources at the national, state, and local levels to address contemporary problems more successfully.

Attempts to improve relationships between community residents and the police, to reduce fear in the community, to enhance problem-solving skills, and to encourage police to better know and respect the communities in which they work are admirable, and research has indicated some positive results of such efforts (Catalano, Arthur, Hawkins, Berglund, & Olsen, 1998; Howell, 1998). But one contradiction that must be reconciled is the vast difference between the popular rhetoric of "community policing" and the reality of strained and even murderous relationships that exist between police officers and many city youth, especially those who are black. An aspect that must also be dealt with concerning this relationship is the fact that both sides feel like victims, the ones being beaten down.

POLICE, FAMILIES, AND YOUTH

At the city police station, after submitting to the customary metal detector scan and X-ray of my book bag, I attempted to set up interviews with officers. In the lobby of the vast building, I met with several officers around a coffee machine. I told them the police officers I knew, including those who worked in Brandon High, and that I was interested in interviewing them about violence in the city. They took the news in an almost amused way but seemed to want to be helpful. After requesting interviews and setting up times, I chatted with them about city problems associated with violence. There seemed to be consensus among them that violence could be defined in three ways: domestic violence, street violence (including gang violence), and violence against the police. One explained: "You get domestic violence and various forms of family abuses. You get the gang-bangers. And then there is the violence I have to worry about—getting shot, beat up, even verbally abused on my beat."

Another police officer explained that violence against the police was common, but nobody paid it much attention because the stereotype and news publicity only harped on images of police officers abusing and shooting citizens. While no doubt partly responses to nationally known accounts of police brutality, the officers' responses also reflected the realities of their jobs and circumstances. To recognize that officers feel alienated from the community and are at times abused and assaulted does not imply that they do not abuse their own power. One officer put it this way: "Usually it's nothing more than verbal that I get from people. I'm harassing them, I don't have the right to do this, I'm a son-of-a-bitch, things like that. It's rare that it gets physical but it does." Another police officer explained, "I've been pushed, shoved. Nobody has physically come after me, against me, but I've been in situations where the person has a weapon—that weapon can be a beer bottle—and they are refusing to put it down. That scares the hell out of me."

This same police officer described a situation that highlighted the isolation and danger that some officers felt in Brandon city. In an interview at his house in a primarily working-class Irish section north of the city, he told me the following story:

> One time I was in a drug area [near Brandon High] and as I pulled into a parking lot of the projects, I saw two males and I observed an exchange. I then decided I was going to approach them and find out what they were doing, if they lived in the area, and begin my investigation that way. Well, as I approached the two males, one went one way and took off and the other went around my patrol car the other way. My radio was an old kind, so I didn't have a shoulder mike. The radio was busy, people were talking so I couldn't tell anybody where I was at or what I was doing. As the one went around my car I got out and said, "Hey, you come here. I want to talk to you." He kept walking. I repeated myself, then he turned and faced me and I saw that his hand was cupped behind his leg. Initially I thought it was because he had drugs. Then he turned and faced me and

brought his hand out to the side, and he had a 9-inch dagger in his hand. I told him, "Drop the knife." He goes, "No." That automatically makes me a little bit nervous. If an officer is telling you to drop a knife, you should drop the knife. I told him again to drop the knife, and he says "No." At this point we are only like 15 feet apart. The way I was trained is if you are 21 feet apart, that person can rush you and stab you before you draw your weapon. I wasn't getting stabbed so I drew my weapon and I told him again, "Drop your knife." He says, "Put your gun away first." It seemed like he wasn't even intimidated by the fact that I was pointing a gun at him and if he had come toward me I was going to shoot him. This was right after the cop was killed in [a neighboring city]. Right after that happens you always become a little more nervous. Eventually he ran into the apartments.

By this point my adrenaline is going and I'm sure his adrenaline is going and the radio air finally broke so I called out on the radio where I was, that I got a man with a knife and I needed help. I chased him into the basement and he went flying through an apartment door and now I hear yelling and screaming in there so now I had no other options. I have to go in because I don't know what's going on in there so I went through the door, knocked people over, and I saw him run around the back corner of the bedroom. I ran back there and he was trying to climb out the window so I told him to stop. He turned around and faced me. He started to come toward me again. I still had my gun drawn because I'm dealing with a person with a knife and I ran toward him and threw him to the ground. When I put him to the ground, I told him to put his arms out. When he put his arms out I saw that he didn't have a knife in his hand so I figured the knife is either underneath him or he dumped it somewhere along his route, so I'm thinking, "OK, his hands are out, I'm safe."

But as I begin to re-holster to handcuff him I realize the people are no longer yelling about him running through, they are yelling at me because I have no right to be in their apartment and now they are all converging on me and now I'm really getting scared. I think he still has the knife underneath him, or I have to assume he still has it. People are yelling and screaming that they want to get me and I'm alone. I get on my radio again and tell everyone where I am. I'm in the basement and I need help. I had no right to chase him they are saying—the people in the apartment. So I put my foot on his back to keep him down and I'm yelling at him not to move because I'm in such a bad position. I did not finish putting my weapon away. I was so scared my foot was vibrating on this guy's back and he realized how scared I was, which made him realize he is not in a very good position. So he began to yell and scream at the people, "Leave him alone, leave him alone, you are scaring him. Don't scare him." He didn't want me to flinch or something like that and at that point my backup came. That was a scary thing—mostly scary because everybody, even the people in the apartment, was against me.

This police officer, like others, felt that he was put into dangerous situations not only because he was in contact with criminals each day but also because people—friends and cousins of criminals, as well as everyday citizens—thought the worst of cops and therefore gave very little support and help. One officer remarked that even the relatively insignificant job of writing parking tickets could turn confrontational: "People don't like it when they get a ticket and they see me and say something like 'Is this all you do with your day—harass people?'" Another officer said that when he tries to intervene in potentially violent situations people say he is harassing. He was part of the Direct Deployment Team, a branch of the city police department. His job was to use local laws and ordinances to question loiterers, people with open alcohol containers, and noise-makers. He told me, "They'll be people in the street shouting at each other. I come up and the people are like, 'Hey, quit harassing us, we're just talking.'"

In addition to their isolation from city residents, many police officers felt isolated from the court system. They felt that too often cases were dismissed or pleaded out, or charges were dropped to lesser offenses. The police officer who described the incident involving the pursuit explained that the individual he arrested was charged with possession of a weapon (the knife) and menacing and obstruction of governmental administration for fleeing, but that ultimately the case was dismissed. With a bit of anger in his voice, he explained:

> Well, he did go to jail. I arrested him and he couldn't post bond, but the judge dismissed the charges and he walked away. I never even got called in for court, they just dismissed it. The Assistant District Attorney contacted me and wanted to let me know the case had been dismissed. I don't know how they dismissed it but they did.

Other officers detailed similar situations: They arrested criminals, they did their jobs, they sent people "downtown," and, in the words of one, "they're walking out the door before I am." One officer explained the relationship between police and the court system as follows:

> It's almost like some officers are indifferent: "I did my job, that's all there is to it." If you start thinking about, "Oh, gee, they are just go-

ing to throw it [the case] out anyway," don't even bother coming to
work, because you are not going to accomplish anything. But some
officers feel that way—why should they bother. I can only do my
part. There's three parts of the justice system. There's my part, there's
the courts, and then there's corrections. I did my part, I did it right.
It's their turn now. They have to take it the rest of the way. I can only
do what I can do. If you start going out there thinking you are going
to change the world, you are going to go crazy because you are not
going to. The criminal goes in front of a judge and they're out tomorrow.

When interviewing this police office, I could not help but feel that he
talked about himself in the third person. The "some officers" he described
included himself. When I asked him if he felt the same way as other officers, he told me, in a matter-of-fact way: "I testified at trial twice in four
years on the force—all the other arrests were pleaded out, dismissed,
thrown out, call it what you will." He asked me, "How would you feel?"
And then concluded, "For me, it means the same thing—what I do doesn't
really matter."

In spite of the power they wield, police officers are not often held in
high esteem by the individuals in the neighborhoods where they work. In
addition, they know that they are the street grunts for the criminal justice
system. As mentioned before, they pick up the slack when families and
schools fail. Many feel put down, and in some ways they are. They are
given the dirty work, and in spite of some initial good intentions, they
are socialized and expected to be the muscle and clean-up crews for city
politicians.

A SYSTEM APART

Some police officers feel disaffected on both sides: They feel isolated from
the community they are meant to serve and also alienated by the court
system, which does not, according to some, support their work. By extension, some police develop an attitude about their work: "I do my job, do
the best I can, then go home," one police officer remarked. Partly because
they feel caught in the middle between criminals and the justice system,
and feel overwhelmed and underappreciated by the system and community,
they define their work in narrow terms of arresting. One police officer
noted that when he first started working he talked to people in the neighborhood and when there was a problem he would ask a lot of questions
and try, if the offense was minor, to sort the situation out without arrest-

ing. "Now," he said, "I just get right to arresting. I have no choice. I kind of lost that sensitivity."

While some may view—or wish to view—police as productive members of the community and effective components of the justice system (in a manner conducive to community policing strategies), the Brandon city police that I got to know did not see it that way. According to them, their role was to make the arrest, no questions asked. "I don't ask questions, the questions are for the D.A.'s office," one police officer told me. Their roles were more mechanical than human. Many complained that there was no time to actually talk to people about problems. One officer explained that most of what he dealt with was "silly kid stuff." Imitating a student, he said, "Everyday I go to my school bus and so and so keeps calling me names." He remarked, as if talking to the student, "Sorry. There's nothing I can do about someone calling you names. That ain't my job. Get your parents."

To arrest is one step in filling prisons, and to develop a mentality that views arrest as effective, one must also come to view prisons as effective. In this way, many police officers come to believe wholeheartedly in the system from which they feel disconnected and even abused. While officers will complain about the criminal justice system, all saw the system, including its use of prisons, as the best way to deal with crime. One officer, after describing an arrest he made regarding a theft, said, "Sure, they'll go easy on him but hopefully just the fact that he had to spend the night in jail will get the point across to him that [stealing is] not something he should be doing." When I asked the officer who complained of losing sensitivity and human contact with people what could be done to solve problems of violence, he did not recommend more human contact or greater police sensitivity. He said, "Simple solution would be to build more jails and put the people away that commit the crimes. That way everybody else in society doesn't have to deal with it." When I noted that it appeared that our society was already doing this at an alarming rate, he responded, "Not fast enough!"

Most police do not identify the "root cause" of violence as poor policing or an ineffective juvenile justice system; they do not blame the dysfunctions that they so often describe. Rather, Brandon officers I got to know shifted attention away from the system of which they were a part and blamed, instead, the less powerful city families. Almost always, when I asked them what they thought was "the real problem with violent youth," they responded, "the families."

While accompanying a police officer on his beat in the area around Brandon High I made two visits to houses where complaints of fights were reported by neighbors. The police officer explained that house arguments were very typical of a day on the beat. After leaving both houses, the officer shook his head sadly, asking, "Where is the father? Who takes care of these kids?" He told me: "I go to domestic disputes constantly, the same people over and over again. You go in there, and she hit me, he hit me. 'Well, let's arrest them,' I say. They say, 'I don't want them arrested.' I say, 'What do you want me to do then, I can't solve your problems.' I can arrest people, that's what I do. So I'll do that." Another police officer explained:

> What we got here is not really a kid problem but a family prob-lem—a problem with parents. You have parents that are as screwed up as the kids. Kids just can't raise kids. These parents never even heard of discipline. And the ones that did have all these ideas that they will get arrested if they discipline their kid. They hear stories of parents getting arrested for child abuse because they spanked them but that is all blown out of proportion. You can't abuse a kid. There has to be a limit on a spanking, but you can spank your kid. This is how parents teach kids. If you straighten out the parents, you straighten out the kids. But the first thing that has to be done is that kids need discipline, and I'm not just talking about a nice talking-to, though sometimes that can work. But when it doesn't a kid needs something that keeps in the kid's mind that he shouldn't be doing cer-tain things.

Focusing on discipline in this way—essentially blaming parents for not disciplining their children and linking this to the primary cause of vio-lence—is one means that police use to distance themselves from the com-munity. Families, especially those that are poor, headed by single parents, and African American, are blamed for violence. In this way, a crucial link is secured: Young people are blamed for violence and so are the families of the young people. This, in essence, blames the entire community. In effect, then, as a mechanism of the justice system, officers defined their roles *against* the community, as consisting of making arrests, and reiterated even when talking about families the effectiveness of harsh (and sometimes cor-poral) punishment. In doing so, they aligned themselves with forces of dis-cipline, not justice.

Some police respond to the alienation they feel—which they them-selves take part in producing and maintaining—by drawing closer to each other and establishing a culture that values toughness and emotional de-tachment, a culture that is self-enforced through a "blue code of silence" (Marans & Schaefer, 1998). Such detachment and alienation have been reported by other researchers, who have identified police training, with its emphasis on codes of confidentiality and "traditional quasi-military criteria," as another way that police officers become cut off from the community (Van Maanen, 1973; Yarmey, 1990). Inevitably, the alienation that they feel is a result of their training, their culture of emotional detachment, and their sometimes hostile practices while on the beat. The alienation feeds the antagonisms that exist between police officers and community residents, turning the relationship into a tinderbox of animosities.

POLICE, THE COMMUNITY, AND ANTAGONISM

One afternoon after Brandon High had let out, I accompanied a police officer on his beat on the south side of the city near the school. While driving through the ramshackle streets, the police officer showed me the new technology in his cruiser, including the laptop computer affixed to the dashboard of the car, which replaced the traditional CB-style radios. The computer was used to file reports and to communicate with other police officers and the police dispatcher. Like the new shoulder mikes the computer solved the problem of air time: the inability of police officers to find open air time during incessant calls on the old CB-style radios. In addition, the officer noted that the new computer system prevented people with shortwave radios from listening in on their calls.

As we passed groups of mostly African American boys standing around pay phones and street corners in front of fast food restaurants, the police officer pointed out the various gang members that operated on the south side: the 2–12s, the 1–10s, and the Bricks. Demonstrating the connection between gangs and turf, each of the names represented addresses. 2–12 and 1–10 referred to block addresses and Bricks referred to the (mostly brick) facades of the projects where the boys lived. Demonstrating, as well, his dislike for the boys and his crude sense of humor, he called them "hood rats," referring to the hooded sweatshirts ("hoodies," the students called them) that they wore.

After arriving at the scene of a church burglary—which turned out to be a false alarm—the police officer was called to a street fight at the Neighborhood Community Center. In an effort to get to the scene quickly and to demonstrate to me the excitement of police work, the officer turned on his lights and siren, floored the gas petal, and turned sharply to the right down a rutted street. I had been sitting in the front passenger seat of the car, but was suddenly thrown across the seat—I smacked my arm against the new computer and almost ended up in the lap of the police officer. Weeks later, I found out that this episode had become police gossip. On two occasions, I was asked by police officers if I was the same person who had almost busted the police computer and had tried to sit in the cop's lap during an emergency call. After I requested an interview from one, he said, "Sure, as long as you keep out of my lap—no funny stuff."

We flew down the potholed city street at highway speed (while I grappled to secure my seat belt), passing individuals who watched us expressionlessly. It seemed that the racing police car with lights flashing and sirens blaring was nothing new to the people standing outside. We arrived at the scene just as the fight ended. The police officer, who was the first to arrive, quickly got out of his car and approached a group of African American youth. He seemed relieved to find one adult among them. The group was standing next to a school bus with a smashed window. Glass littered the ground next to the front right wheel and one boy, standing nearby, was carefully picking shards off his jacket. The police officer asked what had happened and the adult in the group, who was a basketball coach, explained that a group of kids had attacked them as they came out of the community center after a basketball game. In short, the group of basketball players was from the east side of the city, and when a south side gang—the Bricks—found out that the east side team was at the center, they had come to start trouble.

The coach said, "They were waiting for us outside. We tried to create a human chain to protect the kids but it was too scary. We tried to run for the bus, but as soon as we came out, they attacked." Some of the basketball players managed to get on the bus; others ran. Some of the Bricks had rushed the bus and got on before the driver could close the door. One Brick had smashed the window of the bus with a trophy he had taken from the community center trophy case. Though the Bricks had fled, many of the basketball players remained on the bus.

One player, who had gotten on the bus after being attacked, noticed that he was bleeding from his back. The police officer went on the bus and escorted this boy down the stairs of the bus and lifted up his shirt. It looked as if he had been stabbed, though the wound was not very serious; the boy was able to walk. The police officer retrieved rubber gloves from the trunk of his cruiser, put them on, and cleaned the wound with materials from his first aid kit. An ambulance arrived and the medics put the boy on a stretcher and took him to the hospital. Apparently, the boy had been jabbed with a sharpened pipe.

After other police had arrived to take down a report, the officer and I followed the ambulance to the hospital to get a statement from the basketball player who had been injured. On the way, the officer told me that he had been in the Gulf War, had hated the military, and so decided to become a cop, but said, "This is worse, though. It would be better to be in the army." He was in his mid-20s, white, articulate; he cursed constantly, and had three kids of his own at home.

In the hospital emergency room, he asked the boy who had been stabbed routine questions about the attack. The boy's brother, who was the assistant coach of the basketball team, had ridden in the ambulance and sat next to the boy's gurney looking nervous and worried. The boy who had been stabbed insisted to the police officer that he did not know who attacked him. The officer closed the curtain to the room and asked the boy again, "Are you sure you don't know any of the kids, the kid who stabbed you? Maybe now that we are alone, you may remember one of the kids." The boy shook his head and said he did not recognize anyone. He said that he did not even know he was stabbed until he got on the bus and felt the blood on the back of his shirt. He insisted, as well, that he did not know if the group were gang members—though everybody else did.

Later, when a police photographer came to take pictures of the wound and a doctor arrived to check on the boy, the doctor closed the curtain again. The police officer went to talk to a reporter and the police photographer left. It was at this point that the boy admitted that he knew the attackers were Bricks because they had been chanting "Bricks, Bricks, Bricks" just before they charged. The brother, too, who did not say anything to the police officer, noted that they were "Brick city kids." Later the doctor told the police officer what the boy had said, and the police officer offered this to me as an example of networking between police officers and hospital staff. It was also an example of youth not trusting and not cooperating with the police, even when they were innocent victims of crimes.

Mistrust of the police among African Americans and other nonwhites is felt in the projects and on ghetto streets, as well as in middle-class households and neighborhoods. In their research, Weitzer and Tuch (1999) noted that middle-class African Americans were often the most critical of police. Anderson (1990, p. 201) pointed out that even law-abiding citizens were at times reluctant to call the police because they felt that the actions of some officers would be worse than the behaviors of those they wished to report.

From the perspective of police, though, they were the ones being abused and misunderstood. One officer, reflecting the sentiments of others, insisted that there was "a lot of anti-cop feelings with kids, which is a kind of built-in prejudice against police." Another officer explained that it was very difficult to investigate homicides because individuals who witness crimes are often users or dealers of drugs, and if they are not, there is still "an ethos in the community that says it is not cool to talk or cooperate with the police." He said, "Nobody likes cops and that's what leads to the 'us' versus 'them' mentality." It is also likely that animosities are the result of race antagonisms, since most police in the city are white and most kids with whom they deal are not. This animosity was exposed even during times of cop humor. One day, driving past a group of 4- and 5-year-old black children playing on the sidewalk, one boy looked up at the police car and timidly waved to the white officer. The police officer waved back but mumbled to me, "Still young enough to wave to us with all his fingers."

COMMUNITY AND POLICE CROSSFIRE

The animosities that exist between police officers and community residents go both ways: City folk dislike the police and the police dislike city folk. In community meetings when police were present, often one of the topics on the meeting agenda pertained to improving community and police relations, which usually became a very heated and contentious debate. In the summer of 1999, without warning, the Brandon city police chief resigned, and though he stated personal reasons for his decision, many felt his resignation was caused by escalating community-police tensions after the shooting death of a black youth by a white police officer. In discussions with students and some parents, many complained of police bullying and harassment. One student, when asked about the benefits of the DARE program at Brandon High, smirked and shook her head. She explained that police were "about arresting not helping." She highlighted her point with the following story:

> I was coming back from church one time with friends and we got stopped. The police came over and started with us. It was about 8:30 and it was just starting to get dark. We were just hanging, walking home and hanging. We were doing nothing. And the cops come over and say, "Get on the car." And they got the guys on the car. Not the girls. They started searching all the boys. And I said, "Can I just get my hands over here [she makes a movement]?" and they were like, "No, you stay just the way you are." They didn't have nothing on us. We were just hanging. That happens a lot. They stripped this boy for something, one time. He was just coming out of the store and they stripped him down to his boxers. It was winter. I saw it happen.

Another student explained:

> If you are black and you are male, and your wear the big hood, and you're walking down the street, you'll be hassled. Even if they don't find no dope, no marijuana or drugs or anything, and you got money, they'll take it. That's not right. They don't know if you got a job or something. They just think, "You can't have a job." And they

take it [the money]. And another thing that happens, if you are driving a nice car, they always harass you.

Parents too noted the tensions that have developed between the police and especially young black students. I met one parent in her home after her son had been put in Brandon High's afternoon school program because of fears (on the part of school staff and the parent) that he would be attacked by rival gang members in day school. While the parent was concerned about her son's fate in afternoon school, she was equally concerned about policing in the city, which she felt was causing more problems than it was solving. She explained:

> There's more to it than just school and what the schools do. Police too. My kids have never had good experiences with the police officers. One police officer told my kid, "Where'd you get this coat from? Your mom can't afford nothing like this." They think he'd stole it. One time my son was just running, some friends were running so he started running too—kind of crazy, but kids do crazy stuff—and they [two police officers] brought him home in the police car. Police threw him up against the car, they harassed him. You could just be walking. They harass and say, "Ain't nobody gonna believe you, son."

This same parent complained that her son, who had witnessed a shooting on the south side of the city, was "slammed up against the wall and slapped" when the police questioned him about the shooting. "They thought for sure that he knew who did it—a rival gang or something—but he didn't know because I asked him later, and he is truthful, always truthful."

Three police officers I spoke to admitted that they had been charged with police harassment, but to them these were examples of how community members always thought the worst of them and overreacted. However, not all officers felt that there existed poor community-police relations, at least not all the time and not between all cops and all city residents. As Herbert (1998, p. 344) explained, "Discussions commonly treat police subculture as if it were a more-or-less cohesive whole. Cops are constituted as a distinct social group, a coherent 'we' in contrast to the 'they' of the broader public." Some Brandon city police officers made efforts to get to know people and to attend community meetings. In addition, in areas where crime was a significant problem, they set up trailers or "satellite stations" where residents could report a crime or file a complaint. Officers rightly claimed that the trailers were less threatening and more conveniently located than the downtown station. The police department also used the trailers to collect food and clothing for the community. The department referred to these trailers as "community storefronts" and, again, insisted that their main purpose was "community relations."

When relationships are poor between police and the community, we must look beyond "police culture" and examine what Herbert (1998, p. 361) called "normative orders." These are six entities that structure the worldview of police: the law, bureaucratic control, adventure/machismo, safety, competence, and morality. According to Herbert, each shapes the perspectives and behaviors of police. But in addition to these six, I would add "policy," especially zero tolerance. In Brandon city, the police department referred to zero tolerance in their own language of "pro-arrest policies." One day when I was at the police station a detective showed me statistics demonstrating that reports of domestic violence in the city had been decreasing since they had instated a well-advertised pro-arrest policy. But he also noted that police officers have seen an increase in the severity of the violence against domestic partners. I asked him why, and he looked at it logically: "Individuals who know they are going to be arrested and convicted to the fullest extent of the law have nothing to lose by beating their partner more severely."

The detective explained, as well, that the reason for the decrease in reports of domestic violence may be that individuals (mostly women) were hesitant to call 911 because they knew that their partners would be arrested and prosecuted to the fullest extent of the law, which some did not want. He said that many in the police department thought that the pro-arrest policy was not only ineffective but also a cause of greater violence and, in addition, greater anti-cop sentiments.

In reality, the antagonisms that exist between officers and residents of the city are caused by several factors: insensitive and sometimes brutal police officers; negative stereotypes of both police and mostly poor and African American families; and the division of labor that has detached policing from human interaction and justice. While community policing is a step in the right direction, additional police training and various kinds of satellite stations are not likely to close the rift. In addition, citizens and police departments must work to undo anti-humanistic policies such as zero tolerance. We must expect more from police than a manner that is emotionally detached, arrest-oriented, and historically tied to adversarial relationships between law enforcement, youth, and families.

FROM STREET BEAT TO SCHOOL POLICE

The officers discussed in the next two chapters also went about their days with feelings of isolation. Even when they were denying or trying to overcome them, feelings of detachment shaped their ways of doing their work. At Brandon High, the school police officer often explained his role, almost naturally, within an outsider context. He claimed that part of his job was "community relations" and noted that part of the reason he was in the school was to "show these kids that we aren't all corrupt and harassing people like Rodney King." These kinds of defenses were a part of his way of describing his job.

Likewise, Officer Esposito, the police officer who taught the DARE program at Brandon High, explained that one of the most important parts of his job was "fostering good relations with the community." He explained that the most difficult part of the job was working with "so many kids who feel that we [the police] are the bad guys." He explained to me in an interview:

> At the high school level, what I think actually works best is the community relations aspect of it. The kids get a chance to know the police. My purpose for coming here [Brandon High] is not to try and find out who is doing what because once I do that my credibility is gone and they [the students] are going to have more of a disliking for the police. All kids tend to think police are corrupt. And the police have their own perceptions, as well. The police sometimes joke about DARE, they call me the Kindergarten Cop. Police, just by their nature, are more like macho-type people. They think of it more like you are a teacher now and not a police officer. On the other hand, they want to know if all I do is break up fights. I think a lot of police see—especially if they work days—kids of high school age out doing the wrong things. But these are the kids who aren't in school. Really, in schools, you have a bunch of good kids and a few criminal types, but most police think just the opposite.

While school police officers express the same kinds of concerns as their partner street cops, the environment of the school is very different from that of the street. Officers on the street are often in touch with each other, stopping to talk and meet in parking lots to chat and to network. On the other hand, school police officers are usually alone amid individuals such as teachers, students, counselors, and school administrators. They cannot stop to chat with other officers. In addition, school police work for many hours each week with adolescents, some of whom are excellent students and some of whom are difficult if not emotionally destroyed. Officers in schools must foster relationships with students that city police cannot—or will not. In many ways, the role of school police officers reflects that of city cops, with its associated antagonisms and feelings of alienation. Yet the new environment of the school, the incessant contact with youth, the replacement of the police car with an office and hall-wandering (rather than "cruising"), and the fact that the officer must answer to both a police department and a school district add new dimensions to the cop role.

CHAPTER 5

Policing the Urban School Crisis

The development of school policing since its first use in Flint, Michigan, in 1958 is relatively new and therefore has not received much attention. While seen largely as an outcome of policies of the 1950s, school policing is also an extension of 19th-century truant officers and reform schools, which secured the link between a developing public education system and the growing criminal justice system (Tyack, 1974, p. 33). It is also one component of a more expansive police liaison with schools that includes DARE and Police Athletic League (PAL) programs, networking through central offices, and the use of police officers to conduct anti–substance abuse and violence-prevention lectures in schools.

Though Detective O'Hara's job had much in common with those of officers in other schools, the specific roles and expectations of school police are as different as school districts themselves. Some districts refuse to permit school policing (though this is becoming more rare). Others permit policing but are against armed police officers. Smaller cities often hire school officers from the city police department, as did Brandon High. Other cities develop special school police forces, as in New York City, which formed its own 3,000 member Division of School Safety (Ravitch & Viteritti, 1997, pp. 22–23).

Policing in schools gained congressional support with a 1998 amendment to the Omnibus Crime Control and Safe Streets Act of 1968 (PL 105-302). The amendment was enacted to establish school-based partnerships between local law enforcement agencies and local school systems "by using school resource officers who operate in and around elementary and secondary schools to combat school-related crime and disorder problems, gangs, and drug activities" (p. 2841). Reflecting efforts to promote community policing initiatives, the amendment encouraged officers "deployed in community-oriented policing" to work in collaboration with schools and neighborhood organizations in order to

1. Address crime and disorder, gangs, and drug activities affecting or occurring in or around an elementary or secondary school.
2. Develop or expand crime prevention efforts for students.

3. Educate likely school-age victims in crime prevention and safety.
4. Develop or expand community justice initiatives for students.
5. Train students in conflict resolution, restorative justice, and crime awareness.
6. Assist in the identification of physical changes in the environment that may reduce crime in or around the school.
7. Assist in developing school policy that addresses crime and recommend procedural changes.

In spite of the language that promotes communal efforts, the Brandon High police officer explained that many cops do not want to work in schools: "In the school, you live by two sets of rules: the law and the school policies. You have to be able to have rapport with students and live in both these worlds." He claimed that most police find this too frustrating and end up, according to O'Hara, being "strictly cops."

That officers end up being strictly cops is an economic and organizational issue as much as a cultural one. Detective O'Hara was an employee of the city police department and therefore had to adhere to the codes and regulations of the organization that paid his salary. In addition, his training was in law enforcement, not education; therefore he brought to his job police regulations and expectations, and a police culture that was shaped by training and informal codes of behavior acquired over time.

In addition to the professionalized and clinical discourses of the counselors, psychologists, and social workers, which have relied on medical and behaviorist models for the treatment of aggressive students, police bring into school a criminal justice approach to violence prevention. To the medical and behavioral models are added heightened judicial and law-enforcement paradigms that cast students not as "antisocial," "SED," or even "psychotic," but as *criminal*. Examined in this chapter is the role of Brandon High's police officer, specifically how this role was divided into two parts: that which promoted traditional law-enforcement practices (being "strictly cops") and that which required support for students.

THEORETICAL FOUNDATIONS OF SCHOOL POLICING

Most literature that examines the role of school police officers falls into two categories. First, there are discussions about the benefits of school policing. This literature generally acknowledges the advantages of a broad range of liaisons between schools and the police, such as summer academies, drug-awareness and PAL programs, and DARE classes. By extension, school police are another benefit that schools can reap, and in many cases are necessary when schools become sites of attacks. In their national study of school violence, Petersen, Pietrzak, and Speaker (1998) concluded that the most effective school violence-prevention strategies were the placement of monitors and guards in hallways, police liaisons with schools, and a specially trained, positive police force. In another article, one high school police officer explained his role as follows:

> It is our goal to concentrate on prevention, not on reacting to problems. With prevention, our arrest rate has decreased because the students know that school is not the place for criminal behavior. Some of the measures for deterring such behavior include I.D. cards; the use of drug-sniffing dogs in the locker areas; the installation of uniform locks on lockers with a master key held by the administration; and the development of a community service program designed by the Metropolitan School Board, Juvenile Court, and the Metropolitan Police Department. (Holmes & Murrell, 1995, p. 63)

The writings that favor using school police officers can be broken down even further: those that favor police officers but not armed police officers; those that favor school officers who act like city police officers whose main duty is to enforce the law; and those aligned with the community policing movement (see, for example, Bushweller, 1993; Holmes & Murrell, 1995; Skelly, 1997). This final subcategory, literature that supports a more partnership-oriented approach to school policing, reiterates calls for city community policing (Hylton, 1996). A school police officer—or what is called in this case a "juvenile aide worker"—described community policing in schools by noting its attachment to the larger efforts of town and city law enforcement:

> Community policing is a philosophy of law enforcement in which police officers and private citizens work together in creative ways to help solve contemporary community problems, including crime, fear of crime, social and physical disorder, and neighborhood decay. In the process, police departments develop new relationships with law-abiding people in the community, allowing them greater voice in setting local police priorities and involving them in efforts to improve the overall quality of life in their neighborhoods. In return, the police form closer bonds with the community through the development of structured, working partnerships. (Skelly, 1997, p. 26)

But community policing was not developed *by* school police or *for* school police. It was initiated by city police departments, aided by federal grants, to attend to (some would say to gloss over) the realities of police harassment, racially motivated arrests and shootings, and community distrust of police described in the previous chapter. Individuals who approach the subject from a more critical perspective view school police as a kind of student surveillance and even oppression. While there is little literature overtly against school police, some researchers and educators have argued that schools use punishment and surveillance in lieu of prevention and humanistic interventions when attending to troubled youth, and that school policing is an example of this problem.

Devine (1996, p. 76) made the point that the use of school police for discipline causes students to become "split," in that their minds become the property of teachers and their bodies the property of school police and security guards. Teachers do not "touch" students or deal in any way with their physical impulses, and security personnel do not address issues of the mind, only the "dangerous" bodies of youth. As in Foucault's (1975/1995, p. 25) notions of surveillance and apparatuses of social control, school police officers can be seen as one component of a "lockdown" mentality in schools that also includes the use of metal detectors, automatic locking doors, X-ray scanning machines, and other ways of monitoring and keeping students down. But the submission of students to one mass agent of control is not inevitable; as Devine (1996) also pointed out, school safety officers enter schools and at times fraternize with students, are seen as role models by some students, and in some cases are lawbreakers themselves.

THE SCHOOL POLICE OFFICER

Detective O'Hara not only worked at Brandon High as a school police officer, he also graduated from the school in 1970 and had lived all his life in the city. He was white, urban, street smart, and from a working-class Irish background. Not very tall, rather stocky, he often wore to work light-colored khakis that he complemented with a Daffy Duck necktie. He did not wear a police uniform, though he did wear a holster and gun and walked the hallways with an air of purposeful omniscience that I have come to view as specifically "police." In his neat office in the guidance area he was especially fond of talking about the Golden Age, or—as he put it—the "good days," when Brandon city was a place where "kids ran in the street without getting caught in drive-by crossfire." He claimed that he walked between "a hundred and a million miles each day" through the hallways, the three floors, and the basement of Brandon High: As he viewed it, this was his small way of trying to bring back those days. On a day that I had asked him if I could shadow him during his 7:30 A.M.–5:30 P.M. beat—and after obtaining permission from the principal to do this several times throughout the year—he warned me to bring "my walking shoes."

After attending Brandon High, O'Hara entered the police academy, completed his training, his physical, and his tests, and became a rookie cop. In 1987 he began working as a DARE teacher in the grammar schools in the city. In 1992 he became the police officer in one of Brandon city's middle schools. At the time, all middle schools and high schools in the city were in the process of employing city police officers. In 1994 he returned to Brandon High as the school's police officer.

O'Hara often remarked that Brandon High was no worse than other schools. He told me that most of the conflicts were verbal, involving students harassing each other and teachers. He also claimed that there were very few problems with individual students, but that problems of violence revolved around "groups"—students who were in cliques or gangs. "Most fights became group problems," he explained. He said that there was a lot of taunting and that there were more fights between females than males: "Girls are the real problems." He was especially concerned about gang violence but also explained that "we do not have gangs in the school. We have gang members"—a subtle but important difference.

In general, he felt that the situation of violence in Brandon city was "totally out of control." Regarding gangs, he said, "it is almost impossible to control the gang activity but you can control the members, occasionally." He felt that prevention was an important part of his job but he did not talk about prevention in terms of community policing. Instead his role was to be a connection between the school and police department, a link that was secured by gathering information about individual students: "The best I can do is to try to prevent things before they happen. Most importantly, getting information that keeps me up to date with gang activity— that keeps me on guard, so that I am not at a disadvantage." As a school police officer, he was a member of the School Information Resource Program (SIRP), a component of the city police department that consisted of two sergeants, 18 police officers, and a detective (such as O'Hara) in each of the city's four high schools, seven middle schools, and two alternative schools.

Like city police (and school staff), Detective O'Hara viewed the problem of school violence as an outcome of families' failure to discipline or control their children. The problem was with parents, family life—"latch-key kids, students who arrive home earlier than their parents." He told a hypothetical story of a boy who wanted to go out at night. Part morality play, the story was meant to represent how disorder and social problems occur in the city and then move into the school:

> You have kids that want to go out at night. The parent says "No."
> The boy says "I'm going," and goes out, and the parents do not do

anything about it—do not punish the boy, do not make the boy stay in. So that boy comes to school. A teacher tells the boy not to fool around in class. The boy says "No." The teacher tries to enforce her rule and there is a lot of trouble. Of course there is going to be a lot of trouble, there is a tension here. The student does whatever he wants at home. How is he going to learn to do what the teacher wants at school?

According to O'Hara, problems of violence were the result of lax discipline. Like city cops, he recommended better discipline of students, starting at home and continuing at school. Reflecting on his tough-love philosophy, he thought that the principal was very effective because she was "a hard disciplinarian." But Detective O'Hara was not blind to the realities of some families' lives. In reference to the "latchkey kids" that he sometimes talked about, he also explained that some parents could not afford child care or could not convince their children to participate in after-school programs. On occasion he talked about the strained circumstances of families who "couldn't make ends meet" and tried, as well, to avoid always blaming youth. Regarding gangs, for example, he blamed what he called "the culture of neighborhoods." He told me that "part of the problem is neighborhood. It's where you live. If you live in the 'hood,' you got to join a gang just to protect yourself. Some students don't have a choice—and other students, the good students, just don't have these problems."

Detective O'Hara was trained as a police officer, but unlike city officers he did not discuss his alienation from the community (in this case, the school) or from the justice system. He did complain of the difficultly of negotiating his position as part traditional police officer and part school personnel. He was not as much alienated as "caught in the middle," he explained.

Interestingly, several weeks before the end of the 1998 school year, the principal of the school forced O'Hara's resignation. The explanations for his transfer back to the street were contradictory and were for the most part kept secret. Detective O'Hara said that the principal had never liked him and that she wanted somebody who would be more obedient to her. He also told me that on one occasion she had accused him of racism. During the end of the school year when fire alarms and bomb threats were almost daily occurrences, O'Hara told the principal that it was very possible that it was a black student pulling the alarms. Each fire alarm was outfitted with a dark ink that sprayed as the alarm was pulled, so one could identify who pulled it. He said that even if a student tried to wash the ink off it would leave a light stain for a day or two. Because O'Hara was never able to find an ink-stained hand, he thought that it was because darker skin hid the ink mark better. The principal had included this comment in her letter to the superintendent of schools.

O'Hara was slightly bitter that the police department did not support him better. But in spite of its seriousness, the fire alarm incident does not explain why he was removed, for if he were well liked by the administration, his comment would no doubt have passed with hardly a raised eyebrow. The exact reasons for his removal were not certain even to O'Hara, it seemed, but the episode of the transfer did highlight the reality of O'Hara's position—caught in the middle, as it were, between the school and the police department.

The following section is an excerpt from field notes that tells a portion of O'Hara's day at work. It is a glimpse of how he had to negotiate the contradictory roles of school policing. O'Hara exuded a hard-edged, Irish, and working-class urban manner and his comments were sometimes inappropriate and unfair. But in his actions there were times when he seemed to step away from his police training and misconceptions and become, if not a support for students, then certainly on the side of students in the "us versus them" ethos that was so much a part of the school.

POLICING BRANDON HIGH

Detective O'Hara arrived at Brandon High at 7:00 A.M., which was his usual time to start work. Until school started at 7:45, the building was calm, nearly empty, and quiet except for the clatter of the cafeteria workers arranging trays, tables, and chairs, and administrators chatting in the hallways. O'Hara began his day by reading the city newspaper in his office for both the pleasure of a morning read and to find out if anything had occurred in the city that he should know about—a gang fight, a shooting, a Brandon High student who might have been involved in trouble. After reading the newspaper, he left his office and went to the main corridor near the front doors of the building, waiting for students to arrive. This he did every morning. "Always there to greet them, always there to speak to them," he would say.

At one end of the hallway, near the main office, students in the special education program were on line for the free breakfast program. One African American student called O'Hara over and as we approached, O'Hara told me, "here's the special ed. kids." O'Hara met the group of students, bringing a smile to his face, and greeted each one with a friendly "how y'all doing?" The boy who had called us over wanted to know who I was. He was tall and rather handsome, and supported himself with a metal cane. I told him my name and that I was at Brandon High to study school conflicts. He shook my hand, then another student (a white girl who was very short) also wanted to shake my hand. She asked me, "How you doing?" I told her, "Fine" and introduced myself. Then Detective O'Hara told them that we had to go stand by the front doors. He said, "Unfortunately, I have to get to work." The students seemed pleased to have had the attention, and as we walked away, one called to O'Hara, "Get the bad guys."

On the way to the front doors, O'Hara told me again that the group we had just met were "special ed. kids." He said, "The most important part of my job is having good rapport with all of the students." He seemed pleased to have had the opportunity to show me how he must interact with all students on a friendly basis—that his day was not just devoted to getting "the bad guys." I asked him if he felt that he had good rapport with students and he told me that he did. I asked him what indicated that to him and he said, "It's my job to get along with all students, and, well, I do my job well."

While we were standing in the hallway, the buses were pulling up in front of the school and the atmosphere of the building was suddenly charged with the energy of rambunctious students. The early morning tranquillity exploded with the heavy rumbling of buses and the shouts and enthusiasm of students coming down off the steep stairs and into the school. The students poured into several front doors with book bags slung on their backs, past hall monitors who suddenly appeared from their offices. The students joined friends in the main corridor. There was much noise, yelling, calling back and forth, laughing, and pushing. Girls and boys seemed equally noisy and excited. The hall monitors went right to work, urging students to move along to class. While students seemed to be continually in motion, moving from one side of the hallway to the other, none seemed to disperse.

As we watched students come in, O'Hara was vigilant, darting glances across the group while calling to students to move on to homeroom. One student had taken off his belt and was making a whipping sound with it and O'Hara asked him to put it back on, which the boy did. A girl shoved a set of earphones from her Walkman onto the ears of a friend so that the friend could listen to a new CD. O'Hara saw the Walkman and warned the girls that he would have to take it away if he saw it again. "You know the rules," he said. Students came in wearing baggy pants and baseball hats turned backwards and O'Hara told them to take off the hats. "Hats are not permitted," he said. One student put the hat on his nose and asked if that too was against the rules. Another wearing a Giants hat told him that it was part of his religion. "Hats must be put away," O'Hara said, playing along with the students' jokes but also expressing his impatience. Each boy took his time stuffing the hat into his book bag.

O'Hara saw a student who had been suspended come in the door of the school. His name was Regi. He was black and athletic-looking, and wore a bright Gap jacket and low-riding blue jeans. Detective O'Hara walked quickly to him. Regi saw the detective coming and walked faster in the direction of the bathrooms, which was a common escape route for students. O'Hara called Regi in a sharp, clear shout, but Regi ignored him. O'Hara trotted to catch up with him and when he did he stepped in front of Regi, blocking his way. Regi tried to get around O'Hara without touching him. The officer darted in front of Regi again, clearly attempting to keep some distance between their bodies. They did a kind of dance for a while: Regi trying to get around the detective and O'Hara continually stepping in his way. Both of them were careful not to touch the other. O'Hara kept telling Regi, "Regi, Regi, relax, time out, let's talk." Regi scooted around O'Hara and the officer grabbed his coat sleeve. As soon as he felt O'Hara's hand on his sleeve, he stopped trying to get away and seemed to go limp. Some students had been watching the goings-on, but most did not notice. Some looked quickly, shrugged, and continued their conversations or horseplay.

The school remained noisy and students continued to pack the hallway entrance. Hall monitors moved through the crowd. "The bell is going to ring," one admonished. "You know where you have to be when the bell rings." Some students began moving in the direction of their homeroom classes.

Just outside this crowd, O'Hara spoke to Regi, still holding his coat sleeve: "You were suspended Regi, you must leave the school." Regi shook his head in disbelief. He said, "Why was I suspended?" O'Hara either misunderstood or did not want to answer, and said, "Yesterday." Regi seemed confused and asked, "What?" Then Detective O'Hara said, "OK, let's go talk." Regi relented, and the three of us—Regi, O'Hara, and I—walked to the main office. There, women behind the main desk were busy doing their morning duties: preparing the day's announcements, answering telephones, and getting attendance sheets in order. Detective O'Hara and Regi sat in the conference room in the main office. I stood in the doorway looking in, giving them room to speak, but also close enough to see and hear them. O'Hara spoke to Regi in hushed tones, sternly, pointing his finger at him: "You were suspended," he said. "That means you must leave the school. This is a rule I must enforce. If you do not cooperate, I will call a marked car and you will be escorted out in handcuffs. Do you understand?"

Regi suddenly got up and walked past me, clipping my shoulder, and out into the hallway. O'Hara followed. Regi walked through one crowd in the main lobby, out the front doors of the school, and into the crowd of students still filing into the school now through the "single-point entry" door. It appeared that he had left the school grounds.

O'Hara took his place at the front doors again and watched the students come in. Some students said, "Hello" and "What's up?" to him. O'Hara answered in kind, but also reminded them that they needed to get to class. For O'Hara, this was not only a matter of having students get to where they were supposed to be but also of making room in the corridor so the rest of the students could come in.

Suddenly, O'Hara saw Regi come in the door again, looking very determined to get in. This time, the principal was also in the hallway dispersing students to homeroom, and she and O'Hara approached Regi and blocked his entry. Regi did not try to resist. The principal told him, "Come along," and Regi followed her to the main office. They passed behind the main desk and into the principal's private office. She did not allow me to attend their meeting and she closed the door.

I met O'Hara back out in the hallway. "Off to a good start," he said, referring to the first 20 minutes of the day. He explained that Regi had fought with a girl over something that had been stolen at a party. Apparently, over the weekend, there was a party and his ring was lost or stolen and he blamed the girl. They had gone to peer mediation about it the day before but the mediation did not work. After an hour of discussion with the mediators, Regi insisted that he was still going to fight the girl, so he was suspended. But O'Hara also told me that perhaps the mediation team and the principal were not clear enough with Regi. "They had decided to suspend Regi after the mediation, and had not told him," he explained. In the mediation, they had told him that there were grounds for suspension but had not specifically said that he was suspended. So Regi had arrived at school not knowing for sure that he was suspended.

A few minutes after the principal had taken Regi into her office, she and Regi came out, and the principal walked him to the door. Regi left the school looking very angry. The principal went back to her office without saying anything to Detective O'Hara. By now, more students were filing out of the main corridor and to their homeroom classes. The long, loud bell had rung, drowning out even the shouts of students and squawking of walkie-talkies, and hall monitors were now threatening the remaining students with suspension. Detective O'Hara and I went up to the second floor of the school to the large window near the library. We watched Regi leave the school through the parking lot. O'Hara said, "You see, windows are very important."

Just as we were about to leave the window, a student came in the nearby door and asked O'Hara if he could talk to him for a moment. The student said there was an accident in the parking lot: A car pulling into a parking space hit another car. The boy told O'Hara, "The guy just drove into the car while he was trying to pull into the parking space." O'Hara asked the boy who the person was, and the boy said, "Never seen him before." It turned out that he was a teacher in the school. We all went out to the parking lot. Next to a car with a significant dent in its fender was glass from a broken taillight. Detective O'Hara asked the student, "Did you see it happen?" and the student nodded, and said, "The guy pulled in, hit the car, kept going, parked, and went inside like nothing happened." Detective O'Hara asked, "You saw the whole thing?" The student nodded again. The officer said, "I have to fill out a police report," and we went back inside. He thanked the student and recommended that he get right to class, and that he not say anything about the accident to anyone.

Before reaching his office, we ran into a school coach and social studies teacher chatting in the hallway. Students were in their classrooms, sitting on desks and talking, during the homeroom class period. When the teachers saw O'Hara, they asked him if he knew anything about "the Gray kids." The Gray kids were two sons of a high-ranking police official in the city. The sons had been sought for drug dealing and were believed to be members of a city gang. There was a warrant out for their arrest but the boys had fled and were in hiding. O'Hara and the teachers discussed the case's most recent development, which had been reported in the newspaper that morning: that the police had found one boy hiding in a family member's house. O'Hara told the two teachers that he did not know any more than what they had all read in the newspaper. "It's a shame about these kids," one of the teachers said. On the way to his office, O'Hara told me that the boys had been adopted. "It's a shame for the entire family," he said. During the course of the day, several teachers approached Detective O'Hara with comments about crimes in the city, including details they had read about in the city's newspaper involving the Gray kids. Some were obviously looking for gossip, since they knew that he had ties with the police department's information services.

On the way back to his office, we ran into the student who had reported the accident in the parking lot. O'Hara took him aside to talk to him in private. A hall monitor came over and asked me about the accident, and, not wishing to divulge information, I told him that I did not know what had happened. After talking to the student, O'Hara approached me and said, "I have to fill out a report." Students were still milling about in the hallway but it was much quieter than before. O'Hara approached a group of students by the front doors and told one, whom he knew by name, to get back to class. He did this in a stern yet friendly manner. I asked O'Hara what he had talked to the student about—the one who had seen the accident—and he told me that he was just giving him "a set of brains." This was a common expression of O'Hara's. He explained that the boy was in Evergreen Park late last night and the police had come and taken his name because he was drinking illegally. So he told the student to stay out of the park, to be smart. "Giving him a friendly warning—a set of brains," he said.

In the guidance area, the secretary was talking to a counselor—an African American woman—about the problems with adoptions. They turned to me and brought up the incident with the Gray boys. "That poor family," the secretary said. Then she discussed a program she had seen on the television show "60 Minutes," about "a family, a man and woman, professional people, who adopted two kids, and it was terrible. The kid, the girl was on crack or something. She was actually shown on the program, and she was high on it, whatever it was, right on television, that was obvious."

We talked about adoptions. The counselor mentioned that there were more and more studies being done showing that damage to kids is done in the first 4 years of life. "If you haven't reached them by 4 years, they . . . will have real, real problems. It's like a lot of kids here [in Brandon High]." The secretary explained that that was the point of the "60 Minutes" program: that the family did not see the children's medical records so they did not know that the kids had been physically and sexually abused. "It destroyed their family." Another teacher entered the conversation and said, "It affects the whole family as well. All the kids, the natural kids are affected as well." I felt slightly uncomfortable with the tone of the conversation but found myself drawn into it, and mentioned that "the same kind of thing is going on with a lot of children from war-torn countries that get adopted by people here." The secretary nodded, and said, "Yes, now those kids, they are finding, have great problems that just won't go away."

O'Hara was called on his walkie-talkie by a hall monitor. He dashed out of his office, past the secretary's desk, and into the hallway. By the time I caught up with him he was coming back into the guidance area. I asked him what had happened and he nodded in a knowing way and told me, "Just giving kids a set of brains." Before going into his office, he called to students in the hallway to get to class.

The next hour was relatively uneventful. Detective O'Hara meandered through the halls, picked up trash from the floor on occasion, and checked on classrooms. During first lunch, he stayed in the hallways by the front doors and the lunchroom, just as he did each morning as students entered the school. He told me that we should go "walk the halls" again and that I could finish my lunch as I walked. We went to the third floor, walked each of the corridors, went to the second floor and did the same, then returned to the main lobby. Now that the series of lunch periods had begun, groups of students gathered and talked in the cafeteria, in the hallways outside the cafeteria, and outside the school, usually in racially segregated groups.

Looking out the door windows, O'Hara saw students who had been suspended in the parking lot. "Here we go again," he said as he exited the building. He approached the group and told two of the students—whom he knew by name—to leave the school property because they had been suspended. Both were African American. They were standing outside with their friends, a group of about seven black students, all boys. An African American female was also standing nearby; she was not a part of the circle of boys, though she knew them.

O'Hara told the students again that they must "head up to the street," and pointed to the street outside the exit of the school parking lot. Neither student moved quickly. One student asked, "Why do we have to leave?" And O'Hara told him, "You know why. And you know the rules. I don't make up these stupid rules but I do have to enforce them." The two students said goodbye to their friends with handshakes—giving "pops." O'Hara told them again as they were leaving, "You know, I don't make up these rules, but it is my job to enforce them." As we headed back into the school the officer said, "Just giving them a set of brains."

Inside the school we continued to walk the hallways near the cafeteria. Detective O'Hara saw another student approach the entrance doors of the school and blocked his entry. They were in the front hallway facing each other. O'Hara seemed very determined and was strict with this student, who was, like most of the students trying to gain access, African American and male. "You know where you have to go," he told the student, pointing outside. The boy mumbled something and tried to get around the officer. O'Hara grabbed his sleeve and said loudly, "Wait a minute." Standing chest to chest with the boy and staring him in the eyes, he said, "You know where you have to go. I will get the principal, and you know she doesn't have a sense of humor." The boy said he had to reschedule his screening committee meeting. O'Hara said he would take care of it and that the school would get in touch with him. The student turned around and left the building. When I asked O'Hara what that was all about he told me that this was a student who had been kicked out. I asked him why he was expelled and he shrugged, "He's the kind of kid who doesn't want to be in school." He told me that he was kicked out, was attending another school, and wanted to be readmitted to Brandon High but needed to go through screening. He had had an appointment the previous day but missed it.

Detective O'Hara continued to wander the halls, move students on to class, and at times chat with teachers about crimes in the city. During seventh period, while O'Hara and I were standing in the main hallway, another student came into the school. O'Hara went up to him and told him that he had to leave, that he was suspended. He too was black. After O'Hara had asked him to leave, the student explained that he was no longer out of school, that his suspension period was over. O'Hara wanted to know why he was so late for school then and the boy told him that he was at the hospital. O'Hara let him go but told him to go directly to his class.

The student began walking toward his class, then turned toward the cafeteria and bathrooms. O'Hara saw him and walked after him. The boy saw O'Hara, walked quickly into the semi-crowded cafeteria, and went out the back door into another corridor. We followed and came out the back door, where an assistant principal was talking to a tall African American boy. O'Hara looked both ways up and down the hallway. The student was gone. He checked the men's bathroom for teachers but the student was not there. He checked the men's student bathroom but it was locked. O'Hara turned to me and said. "Did you see what he did? He walked into the cafeteria, knew I was after him, went out the back door and took off."

O'Hara approached the assistant principal, who was still talking to the student. He told him what had happened and the assistant principal shook his head but did not seem very interested. He told O'Hara that he was trying to explain to the student what "guilt by association" meant. He asked O'Hara to explain for him. O'Hara, still angry, tried to shift gears from pursuer to lecturer. He told the student that it was "all a part of who you hang with." The student nodded, smirking. Obviously he knew what they were talking about. O'Hara was strict but casual. He knew it was his job now to give a bit of a lecture—that the assistant principal expected it—and he was playing the role, doing his duty.

He told the student that he should be careful hanging out with Joshua Wright, a student who had been expelled for bringing to school a kind of homemade pepper spray. The student continued to nod, smirking. The assistant principal agreed with O'Hara and told the student that he should listen to him. "He knows the cops," he added, then told the student to get back to class. O'Hara continued to look for the student who had escaped him—it really seemed to irk him that he got away. By the end of the day, as O'Hara left following afternoon school, he had yet to find the student, but he told me as we left for the evening, "There is always tomorrow."

THE ROLE OF A SCHOOL POLICE OFFICER

The feelings of alienation and detachment that accompany city policing do not just enter schools and reproduce themselves without being transformed in some way. School police officers must forge a new role for themselves, one, as O'Hara noted, that is quite difficult for some cops to maintain. While one role borders on being a support for students, the other is confrontational and reflects the reality of policing in the city—white cops versus black males. The context of the environment in which this new role is forged is set within the structure of schooling itself, which includes (but is not limited to) the arbitrary groupings of tracked and special education students determined by professional knowledge and clinical discourses, bells that sound to designate the movement of students, the not-so-impervious partitions between the school and the street, the purposeful limiting of student interactions and expressions through school regulations, and the hierarchical expectations that turn police officers into enforcers of school policies. Through this context, which links school policy, educational theory, and law enforcement, the officer manipulates, and is forced to modify, police training to be conducive to school expectations.

While O'Hara may have at times felt caught in the middle between police and school expectations, he did not express the same strong feelings of isolation that many city officers talked about and demonstrated in their work. He did not work in the citywide community; and in the school he was often accepted by teachers and administrators who saw him as a symbol of control and a means of making their own jobs easier. As responsibilities of discipline and school control have been taken over by police officers, teachers relinquish an unpleasant responsibility: discipline. For teachers and administrators who wished to make their own hectic jobs easier, who were sometimes fearful of violence and generally in need of reassurances that the school was under control, the presence of the detective was a welcome relief.

For a majority of students, the police officer was a built-in part of schooling—a taken-for-granted part of education. Some were critical of the apparent need for the officer but most students seemed to think that the officer and guards made the school safer. These were students who were born in the 1980s and have been raised during two decades of panic about crime, of increased police power, of prison expansion and soaring rates of incarceration, and during the rise of "get-tough" policies. Many can hardly remember a time when there was not a police officer in their schools.

As mentioned earlier, often school policing is seen as another means of social control, enacted by a school system that is obsessed with conformity and regulation. And to some extent, this is true. But O'Hara's days were also punctuated with more humanistic engagements. His role not only involved duties revolving around law enforcement, but also required that he get to know and sometimes help students. It was not atypical that the first two significant occurrences on this day that I accompanied him were a friendly chat with students in the special education program and then a confrontation with an African American boy trying to enter the school.

Bringing to attention more citywide and nationwide realities involving white authority and black youth, as well as the segregated placement of students in special education programs, the scenarios also represented the role of the officer as a kind of juggler of responsibilities.

While O'Hara seemed unaware of the fact that the students in the special education program were so well confined in alternative classes that they seemed almost invisible during the regular school day, he more than others in the school talked to them in a friendly and casual manner. Most of O'Hara's interactions during the day revolved around short chats with students and sometimes teachers. He urged students to get to class and even warned some of potential trouble from city police or school administrators. His visibility in the school as one who "walks the halls" and is not separated from his constituencies by a police cruiser put him in contact with young people in ways that city police, and even some teachers, may never experience.

Rather than suggest that school police officers have to be trained in both traditional police methods and human relations—as community policing advocates suggest—it becomes crucial to view the fluidity with which O'Hara balanced his duties, and therefore the new kind of education that is required. When Regi tried to come into the school, O'Hara was responsible for apprehending him. He told him sternly, "You are suspended. That means that you have to leave the school. This is a rule I must enforce." And when it seemed that Regi was not going to cooperate, O'Hara told him that he would call a marked car and that he would be escorted out of the building in handcuffs. But before the handcuff threat was made, O'Hara tried to talk to Regi. He kept telling Regi to "relax, time out, let's talk." He knew that Regi was very angry, and he was critical of the school for not informing Regi that he had been suspended.

While O'Hara's criticism of the school was mild (he told me that "the school should have been more up-front with Regi"), it must be understood within the context of a person who rarely, if ever, criticized school policies to an outsider. In the end, O'Hara was neither an advocate nor a traditional police officer—he was some amalgamation of the two. He abided by school rules but also criticized them. He allowed Regi to be taken away by the principal but also regretted that the principal, who he knew would be stern, got involved. O'Hara did not take on one role and then another; rather he worked between the two, always part of one enacting another.

ALLIANCES IN UNEXPECTED PLACES

While the detective pursued his police duties, he also distanced himself from the school. His conflicts with the principal—which I did not know about at the time—may have fueled part of this behavior. He explained to students gathering outside the school that he "didn't make the stupid rules. I just have to enforce them." Two of the students had been suspended and were talking with friends during lunch. They were talking quietly and they were not breaking any rules except those prohibiting suspended students from being on school grounds. O'Hara knew the students' names and appeared to know that they were little more than kids who did not always obey school rules. The two students left without incident, and O'Hara explained again to the remaining students that he did not make the rules, wishing, it seemed, to make them understand his intermediary position. After this, he chatted with the students and then suggested that they go inside so that they would not be late for class.

At times, when he was giving students "a set of brains," students were breaking rules that might have led to suspension if they had been caught by one of the assistant principals. While youth-police antagonisms were still present, things were different in the school: Antagonisms were altered because of factors such as O'Hara's sometimes conflict-ridden relationship with the school system itself, his working-class and urban background, and his sometimes macho style that had more in common with students, especially the boys, than with most school staff. O'Hara was caught in the middle, but because of this he was, at times, in a better position to negotiate rules and consequences with students, and therefore to challenge some school policies.

School police officers are an estranged part of both police departments and school systems. As police officers, they cannot always follow informal codes of police culture because policing itself is defined in relation to the street. The street is not a school, regardless of how often staff insist that street problems *come into* the school. In relation to the school system, O'Hara was an outsider, who at times felt more support and camaraderie from students than from administrators. Often, teachers, counselors, and administrators had neither the time nor the sensitivity to make decisions based on understanding and not just school policy. O'Hara did not create and maintain a role that was significantly caring, nonhierarchical, and fair to both students and the school system. But a close look at his daily interactions and duties points to an unexpected reality: He was not just an agent of social control. He also enforced school policy with some reluctance, bent rules, and warned students of potential trouble from administrators.

Regardless of whether individuals approve of the notion, like counselors and psychologists before them, school police officers are becoming increasingly a part of school systems. If we consider *how* they should be a part—and not just *if* they should be a part (for it is too late for that)—we must recognize how their presence in the school must remain separate from the school system while they work in it. Their role must severely challenge police culture while offering the help that law enforcement can provide. Rather than becoming a component of a board of education or even remaining members of police departments, it may make more sense for "school safety officers" to become entities of a community coalition of adults and youth. The community coalition might be part of a larger civic association and could be funded through the Safe Schools Act or the original Omnibus Crime Control and Safe Streets Act, which funds some police officers. Being a part of a strong community group may increase the expectation that officers not only arrest but also act as a check on school systems' often skewed disciplinary actions.

But if officers remain under the authority of the police department, they must continue to abide by the laws that apply to police and not to those that refer specifically to schools. Since the *New Jersey v. T.L.O.* U.S. Supreme Court case in 1985 permitted school authorities to search students when they had reasonable suspicion of wrongdoing and not the higher standard of probable cause, the role of school officers in searching students is murky: must they have probable cause to search students (as do all police officers) or can they as school staff members search a student under the weakened version of the law? While school staff often have capabilities to do to students what police cannot, they do not have the power to slap on handcuffs and to book students. Thus, since police wield great power, constitutional protections must be upheld, including those governing searches and seizures, detainment, and Miranda rights.

FROM SCHOOL POLICE TO CLASSROOM COP

In earlier chapters I focused on violence in Brandon High and how the school responded to it. Different forms of violence and the school's use of a screening committee and police officers have been viewed within the context of the city and of policy, and concerns regarding physical, verbal, and systemic violence in school. What has not been examined is the classroom, and how violence and violence prevention enter into classroom dynamics and influence not only school structures and policing strategies, but also classroom pedagogy.

In the context of DARE programs, police enter the pedagogical realm of schooling and take on the role of teaching, not policing. The DARE program not only brings to U.S. classrooms curricula and instruction that address violence in schools and neighborhoods and alcohol and drug abuse, but it also completes a school-police department counterattack against violence that includes both law-enforcement and pedagogical tactics. What remains consistent with other forms of violence prevention is the conception of school violence as that which can be corrected through cognitive skill development. In general, the DARE curriculum combines didactic lecturing, discussion, role-playing, and problem-solving exercises to help students understand what adults hope they will do when faced with situations involving violence, alcohol, and drugs. But, as in all classrooms, the curriculum does not always go as planned.

CHAPTER 6

DARE Students Speak of Violence

The Drug Abuse Resistance Education (DARE) program at Brandon High was taught by Officer Esposito, who, like DARE researchers, could not be sure that the program actually decreased rates of violence and drug abuse among students: "We really can't be sure if DARE has a long-term effect on kids. That most kids like it and think it beneficial, which we know from our evaluations, is something we have determined."

Officer Esposito was a rather small, thin Italian American who, as a rookie police officer working the night shift, had put in for a transfer to the DARE program, primarily because he wanted to work with young people and could not see himself working the street for the rest of his life. He was one of 15 officers who had put in for the transfer, and it took him 3 years to receive approval. Fortunately, he had been coaching track at North Side High School in Brandon city and therefore knew people in the school system, which, he rightly claimed, helped him to finally get the transfer. Once his transfer was approved, Esposito, and another 20 officers, went through the standard academic preparation for DARE, which entailed a 2-week training period at an upstate New York hotel by a Bureau of Municipal Police (BMP) trainer. The training program consisted of instruction in teaching techniques, mastering the DARE curriculum, and role-playing exercises.

Officer Esposito taught DARE at other schools in the city. At Brandon High, he conducted two 40-minute classes during the third block period. He wore his uniform to classes, including handcuffs and gun, and used Detective O'Hara's office during his free time. He told me that he had once thought of becoming a teacher, but had decided not to after a friend had become a police officer and it occurred to him that financial remuneration would come faster if he went the police officer route.

Behind his police exterior was a person who liked to work with students and felt relatively comfortable in the school environment. He was also a volunteer mentor for an African American third-grader in the Officer Friendly Program, a city initiative that assigned police mentors to elementary school children. He felt that the best part of his day was coaching

track, which he did after school at North Side High. As a DARE teacher
he longed for a city-police relationship that would stigmatize neither the
police nor city kids: "What helps most about DARE is getting to know the
students. Perhaps they get to know me as a person, not a uniform, and I
get to know them as people, not this or that type of kid."

Regarding DARE classes, Esposito thought it was especially important
that students felt they could ask questions. He explained:

> I think my biggest thing is the first day I let them know that I am avail-
> able to answer any questions they have. I don't care if it is controver-
> sial, something you feel may insult the police—this is an educational
> setting. I'm not here to find out what you are doing, if you are doing
> stuff wrong. I don't run people's names to find out if you have a re-
> cord. You are here to learn, I'm here to teach you, I'm a guest. I want
> them to know that. If I have some expertise in police work that I can
> help you with, I'd be more than happy to do so.
>
> I always let them [the students] know that no question is a dumb
> question if you don't know the answer to it. I don't care what you
> ask—I am open in that way. I think the big thing is that they hear
> that and might not believe it but when kids start asking and I actually
> answer their questions [they're amazed]. We talk about things like
> Rodney King and I think kids are shocked when a kid would raise
> their hand and ask that because that's just something you don't ask
> the police.

Embedded in his short description of how he envisioned the DARE
program were the issues that remained prevalent during the two 6-week
programs that I observed: student questioning, controversy, and the violence associated with police harassment and brutality.

Reiterating themes addressed in the two previous chapters, Esposito
noted that students asked questions that revealed their mistrust of the police. Much of what he said about DARE and did in class was tinged with
this awareness. In classes, sometimes there was a subtle hostility in the air,
present in the very fact that a police officer was standing before young men
and women, many of whom were African American and some of whom
had had unfortunate experiences with the criminal justice system. He said
that this was especially true at Brandon High, where many of the students
were what he considered kids who had had "run-ins with the law." In part
because of this self-consciousness and these perceptions of Brandon High
students, Esposito saw himself as a resource person with a neutral approach to handling controversial questions.

When I asked Esposito what the most common questions he received were, he chuckled for a moment, then said:

> There's big ones like what do the police do with the drugs that they confiscate. All kids tend to think police are corrupt. But if you explain the whole process to them, some might have a different view. The first time I got that question I only knew the process I was involved in. I didn't know that the drugs were actually chemically destroyed after. I was a little blank on it and the kids were laughing. The next week I came back with the answer. I went to the crime lab and asked exactly what happened. I let them know that too, that I'm not an expert on everything in the police department. More of a resource that they can find out things from.

In his assessments of classes, Esposito often focused on the students who were the most critical. He made sure I knew that some students "just wanted to create controversy." But he also wanted me to know that some students, including those who were critical, sought advice and information from him, which was something he welcomed. Esposito seemed to bounce back and forth between self-consciousness and enthusiasm. As we shall see, while he cherished the energy that came with some discussions, he did not like feeling on the defensive when talk turned to police corruption and racism in the city. Though the students' questions may have been annoying to him, they were also politicized, critical, and at times sophisticated. The following field note of a classroom observation hints at some of these dynamics.

> Officer Esposito was at the front of the room discussing civil court and custody laws. He asked the class if anybody knew about custody laws. An African American student raised her hand and said, "17% of a guy's salary has to go to child support." She said that she knew this because she had a child, but the father refused to give her assistance and she went to court. A student from across the room—another African American girl—asked, "You got to go to the city court building for that?" The first girl said, "My mother helped me." The second girl then turned to Officer Esposito. "What do I have to do?" Esposito told the girl that she had to take the father to court. "I got to pay for that?" the girl asked. Officer Esposito said, "Not necessarily. Let's talk after class, okay?" The girl nodded, dug into her handbag for a note pad that she jotted in and passed to her neighbor, another African American girl—passing a note, it seemed.

Officer Esposito continued with his lesson. He began talking about the Internal Revenue Service (IRS)—as an example of a federal agency—and noted in his discussion that the IRS may confiscate the assets of those who are convicted of drug dealing. A black girl wanted to know how they knew if the money was related to drug dealing: "What if a family member gave it to him?" Esposito explained that it would still be confiscated because the criminal had not paid any taxes. The girl said that was not fair. She explained: "If the money was related to drugs, it should be confiscated, but if it wasn't—if it was given to them by a family member—then it should be left alone because it has nothing to do with the crime." Officer Esposito said that new drug laws enabled authorities to freeze the accounts of suspected drug dealers. The student insisted that "a person needs to be found guilty first, and even if he is, you should have to make sure that the money is really drug money and not money he got from his family." Officer Esposito conceded that this was a very controversial subject.

Most students became instantly interested in exchanges about criminals and controversial laws, but not all: One African American boy had his head down on his desk and closed his eyes, apparently to go to sleep.

Other questions followed this initial exchange. One white boy who sat at the front of the room asked, "If a dealer puts his money in a foreign account, like a Swiss bank, will the U.S. police still be able to confiscate it?" Before Officer Esposito could answer, another student, also white and male, asked, "If a person breaks the law and then goes across state lines, will the police go after him?" Officer Esposito said it depended on the seriousness of the crime and how far the criminal went. It seemed that Esposito was about to answer the question about foreign accounts when another student, a white female, suddenly asked, "If a criminal comes back to the state where he committed a crime, will you arrest him?" Officer Esposito told the student that the police would arrest the criminal if they caught him. "What if somebody steals a candy bar, or some clothes, and gets away?" another student asked. "Will they issue a warrant for the person's arrest?" Esposito explained that the police would not issue a warrant, but that they would issue a criminal summons.

At this point, a white student unfolded a speeding ticket that he had in his pocket and asked Esposito how much he would have to pay for doing 75 mph in a 55 mph zone. Esposito told him that he was not sure. An African American boy suddenly asked, "When people swear on the bible, do people still lie, you think?" Esposito said that he was sure that some did. At this point, a black girl said that some people are not religious, so it is not a problem for them to lie. Another black girl said that it was against some people's religions to swear on the bible. Another black female said that this could be against freedom of religion—to make someone swear on the bible. Another black girl suddenly said, "My aunt is in prison."

The vignette is short, but already begins to challenge several stereotypes of young people: first, that adolescents are not thoughtful critics of the world and are not politically engaged; second, that students mindlessly resist authority just for the sake of being difficult (and have no justifiable basis for their disagreements); and finally, that students do not want the help or advice of adults. These stereotypes are "truths" that I have heard again and again in Brandon High, in other schools, and in everyday conversations with some adults about young people. But these students, and many students I have met, were curious, politically engaged, and willing to seek advice if adults opened themselves up to giving it in a way that was not condescending. The vignette also points out how classroom interactions were enacted through dynamics of race, social class, and gender, with poorer African American students, and especially females, being the most critical of police ways of doing things.

These are topics that I will return to after a brief overview of DARE in a more national context, and in regard to its curriculum. The development of DARE in the early 1980s, and the policy that mandated its funding, set the context for how the program would be taught and for what reasons. In essence, it provided the backbone for the curriculum. The curriculum was then designed as a kind of "road map" that was meant to be followed by all classes and DARE teachers in the nation. As it turned out, many interactions in the classes I observed were reactions against its straight-and-narrow course.

DARE IN A NATIONAL CONTEXT

Unlike other violence-prevention programs such as peer mediation, which though supported by federal policy are the result of local initiatives that are difficult to track historically, the DARE program has clear beginnings in Los Angeles. DARE was developed in 1983 by a collaboration between the Los Angeles Police Department and the Los Angeles Unified School District. At the time, Darryl Gates, who had once been an adviser to George Bush's presidential campaign on crime and drugs, was chief of police in Los Angeles. Gates's record as police chief is mixed: While he has been charged with organizing and supporting a highly abusive and racist police force that made front-page news throughout most of the 1990s, he has also defied the National Rifle Association by supporting bans on hand-guns and assault weapons and putting his weight behind gun-control legislation when many politicians would not.

In spite of these dubious beginnings, DARE has won the support of the U.S. Congress, which passed the Drug-Free Schools and Communities Act of 1986 (PL 99-570). In doing so, it appropriated federal money for school districts and police departments to develop liaisons that would sustain DARE programs. It also included money for treatment and counseling services, as well as professional development for teachers. It specified that programs sustained with funds from the act would have to teach students that alcohol and drug use was "wrong and harmful." In general, the act made available $200,000,000 in 1986 (and slightly more in following years) for the development of drug and alcohol abuse prevention and education programs, which focused on:

1. The development, acquisition, and implementation of elementary and secondary school drug abuse education and prevention curricula that clearly and consistently teach that illicit drug use is wrong and harmful.
2. School-based programs of drug abuse education and prevention and early intervention (other than treatment).
3. Family drug abuse prevention programs, including education for parents to increase awareness about the symptoms and effects of drug use through the development and dissemination of appropriate educational materials.
4. Drug abuse prevention counseling programs (which counsel that illicit drug use is wrong and harmful) for students and parents, including professional and peer counselors and involving the participation (where appropriate) of parents or other adult counselors and reformed abusers.
5. Programs of drug abuse treatment and rehabilitation referral.
6. Programs of in-service and pre-service training in drug and alcohol abuse prevention for teachers, counselors, other educational personnel, athletic directors, public service personnel, law enforcement officials, judicial officials, and community leaders.
7. Programs in primary prevention and early intervention, such as the interdisciplinary school-team approach.
8. Community education programs and other activities to involve parents and communities in the fight against drug and alcohol abuse.

9. Public education programs on drug and alcohol abuse, including programs utilizing professionals and former drug and alcohol abusers.
10. On-site efforts in schools to enhance identification and disciplining of drug and alcohol abusers, and to enable law-enforcement officials to take necessary action in cases of drug possession and supplying of drugs and alcohol to the student population.
11. Special programs and activities to prevent drug and alcohol abuse among student athletes, involving their parents and family in such drug and alcohol abuse prevention efforts and using athletic programs and personnel in preventing drug and alcohol abuse among all students.
12. Other programs of drug and alcohol abuse education and prevention, consistent with the purposes of this part.

Four years after the original legislation, as part of the Crime Control Act of 1990 (PL 101-647), an amendment to the Drug-Free Schools and Communities Act was passed. The amendment was given the unwieldy title The Drug Abuse Resistance Education and Replication of Successful Drug Education Programs. It read, in part, that "local education agencies in consortium with police departments" would develop drug abuse resistance education instruction in the following areas: drug use and misuse, understanding the consequences of drug abuse, resistance techniques, assertive response styles, managing stress without taking drugs, decision-making and risk-taking, media influences on drug use, positive alternatives to drug abuse behavior, interpersonal and communication skills, self-esteem building activities, and resistance to peer pressure and gang pressure.

The amendment captures the spirit of DARE programs, especially in regard to its focus on resistance techniques, assertive response styles, decision-making and risk-taking, and other strategy-building exercises that are meant to teach students to just say no to drugs and alcohol. The amendment also included provisions for parent involvement, classroom instruction by a uniformed law-enforcement official, the use of student leaders to influence younger children to avoid drugs, an emphasis on activity-oriented techniques designed to encourage student-generated responses to problem-solving situations, and the awarding of a certificate for completion of the program.

As a result of local and national support, DARE programs have been developed in all states in the United States (and in several foreign countries, including England and Australia). They are administered to about 25 million students in 70% of school districts in the United States (Anderson, 1997, p. 337). The original 1983 program was a curriculum for fifth- and sixth-graders and included 16 lessons. The Brandon city school district be-gan their program in 1988 and within a year, in addition to fifth and sixth grades, the district introduced the program into their eighth-grade classes. This curriculum was slightly revised; it had 12 lessons that were meant to be a review of the fifth and sixth grades. In 1990, the high school curricu-lum was written, then in 1991 it was introduced to one high school in the city. It came to Brandon High in 1995 and consisted of 12 lessons for 10th-graders that were taught during health classes twice a week for 6 weeks.

Most studies of DARE are evaluations that attempt to assess the short- and long-term effectiveness of the program. Results are mixed. Most evaluators recognize the inconclusiveness of the research, which is often attributed to the difficulties of accounting for a control group in standard experimental design evaluations. Since schools have seen an increase in all kinds of violence-prevention measures, including peer mediation and char-acter education, even when incidents of violence do decrease, one cannot be sure if it is because of the DARE program or other violence- and drug-prevention programs and messages (Kochis, 1995, p. 42). While some stud-ies found benefits, Kochis observed that of the 12 criminal offenses she recorded in her research, 11 were by five students who had taken the DARE program. This could lead some to believe that DARE may actually cause some violence. Some researchers noted that their results, when dem-onstrating the benefits of DARE, reflected national trends in decreased rates of crime and drug use, and might have been a result not of DARE but of more global patterns (Zagumny & Thompson, 1997, p. 38).

The determination of the "effectiveness" of DARE will always be con-tentious, since one cannot predict outcomes across all gender, racial, and socioeconomic groups. Nor can we "control" the social milieu of students and of the different classroom dynamics and manners of teaching DARE that undoubtably account, at least in part, for its "outcomes." In spite of these evaluation difficulties, it is important to figure out the benefits of DARE, which can be done by examining the educational process itself, for this too factors into whether DARE is beneficial. Regardless of outcomes and effectiveness, the program, like all school instruction, should include stimulating classes that, if conducted well, will help students both socially and intellectually.

In what follows, I examine DARE as a process of education, beginning with its curriculum. While my focus is on the DARE program, the chapter is also an examination of violence from the perspectives of students. What has been, thus far, a bird's-eye view of Brandon High and the city becomes, in the rest of this chapter, a more specific analysis of classroom dynamics. The focus is on how interactions and perspectives on violence are shaped by life experiences and race, gender, and social-class realities. Most significant about DARE classes—at least from my perspective—were the means by which some students displayed an acute interest in information and controversies that revealed their concerns about violence, especially in the context of power imbalances and harassment in the city. Sometimes this was done at the same time that assertions of power and harassment were being enacted in the classroom.

THE CURRICULUM

The student handbook for the DARE program at Brandon High, which was given to each of the students on the first day of class, explained the program thus:

> The DARE program for senior high school has been planned to help you re-view the important skills you learned in the junior high school DARE pro-gram. These skills were designed to enable you to resist peer pressures and to become better decision makers. DARE in senior high school is designed to enable you to recognize and manage feelings of anger without causing harm to yourself or others. You will also have an opportunity to recognize how the use of alcohol and drugs, as well as media influences, contribute to violent behavior. (Bureau of Municipal Police, 1990, p. iii)

In general, the curriculum was the same for each school in Brandon city and throughout the United States. On the first day of class, students took a DARE test to determine how much they knew about violence, drugs, and alcohol, and on the last day, they took a similar test to assess their learning, which some health teachers included as part of students' final grades. On the second and first real day of instruction, students filled in a worksheet from their handbooks that asked them to list drugs' "Effects on Community" and "Effects on Teenagers." After soliciting answers from one class, Esposito wrote them on the board (see Fig. 6.1).

The remainder of the class was used to discuss famous individuals who had died or who had had their careers ruined by drugs and alcohol. The handbook recommended discussing Len Bias, John Belushi, Steve Howe, Elvis Presley, Betty Ford, and Ben Johnson, though in most classes discus-sion revolved around the latest professional athlete who had been punished for cocaine or steroid use. On the third and forth days of class, students role-played strategies for turning down drugs and alcohol. The next 2 days were spent learning about federal and state laws and school codes regard-ing violence, drugs, and alcohol. From here, students learned about the effects of intoxication on the body and went over a chart that explained blood-alcohol content according to body weight.

Figure 6.1.

Effects on the Community	Effects on Teens
1. Violence	1. Suicide
2. Crime	2. Homicide
3. Lose money	3. Car accidents
a. taxes	lose money
b. welfare	overdose
c. dealing and buying	rape
d. jail	
bad reputation	
child neglect	

DWI . . .

During the next 2 days, students read "real-life" scenarios regarding alcohol, determined the blood-alcohol content of the characters in stories, and discussed the decisions that they would have made if they had been the characters in the scenarios. In one of these scenarios, for example, a daughter noticed that her father had been drinking more after being laid off from work. One afternoon, she found six empty beer cans in the garbage pail that her father (who weighed 170 pounds) had just finished drinking in the last 2 hours. Students were asked to determine the father's blood-alcohol content, then discuss what they would do if they were the daughter. Combining "scared-straight" tactics, cognitive skills development, and decision-making strategies, the exercises were meant to combine the intellectual and the social, and also to be relevant to high school students' lives.

Following these exercises, students discussed differences between federal and civil courts. The next 2 days were spent working on real-life scenarios again, this time involving violence. In one scenario, the following incident was explained:

Carlos and Jennie were attending a birthday party for Carlos' cousin. It was getting warm inside the hall, so they decided to walk outside to the parking lot. Several cars were cruising up and down the street. A teenage male in one of the cars called out to Jennie to come get into the car. Carlos became very angry and felt the need to defend Jennie. He shouted back at the teenager in the car. Then someone in the car pointed a gun at Carlos and fired several shots which nearly hit both Carlos and Jennie. What choices do Carlos and Jennie have? (Bureau of Municipal Police, 1990, p. 39)

Below the scenario, three columns were given in the workbook. The header for the first column read *Choices*. The next two columns were labeled *Gains* and *Losses*. For each choice that Carlos and Jennie could make, students were asked to identify the possible gains and losses. The first row was already filled in for students by the handbook's manufacturer. It read under *Choices*, "Notify his homeboys and get even." Under *Gains*, it read, "Revenge"; under *Losses*, "May get killed." Students were asked to add three more rows, explaining the choices and the consequences ("Gains" and "Losses") of those choices. After this, students were asked "How could the situation have been avoided?"

Students completed several of these scenarios in the workbook. All of them described potentially violent situations. After this, they were given a list in their handbooks of "Nonviolent ways to deal with conflict situations":

1. Treat other person with respect.
2. Listen until you experience other's point of view.
3. Stay in control. (Don't allow anger or fear to put you on the defensive and be forced into fighting.)
4. Keep calm. (Keep voice low and refrain from name calling or swearing to keep situation from intensifying.)
5. Put yourself in other person's place. (Think about how he or she feels or thinks.)
6. Give other person a way out or chance to "save face." (Don't force person into a position where he or she has no other alternative but fighting.)
7. Apologize or give an excuse. (Apologizing is a simple way to avoid or diffuse a conflict. Apology does not establish who is right or wrong.)
8. Use humor. (Using humor appropriately oftentimes helps to keep a situation from escalating into a serious situation.)

On the last day of class Esposito asked students to fill out an evaluation of the program. Based on a sample of 50 evaluations that I reviewed, the most common reactions to the program by Brandon High students were that Officer Esposito was well informed; that the role-playing was fun; that the program should have included guest speakers/peers/experts to share their experiences of police work and prison; that Officer Esposito had interesting stories and that he should tell more stories about what happens on the street/in courts/in prisons; and that it would be good to have people who have been arrested come to speak to the class. One student wrote as a comment: "Give more information on our rights and not just the laws."

In general, most students liked the class. Many students claimed that Officer Esposito was easy to talk to and some said the program should be longer. As noted earlier, some viewed the program as a way to get helpful information involving domestic abuse, harassment, and gangs. One black student, a ninth-grader who had just left home and was living with her boyfriend, shared her own experiences in a second- and third-person account when she explained to me:

> I think the DARE class can be helpful and good sometimes. It was. Like some girls in our class was probably having trouble with their boyfriends. They probably wanted to know how they can deal in a good way without getting themselves hurt and the man hurt—just to get away from him. Because a lot of people in this school don't have a person to talk to. You can talk to him [Officer Esposito]. Because he wasn't like one of them other cops that seem like they are higher than us. He just seemed like he was down with us. He knew exactly what we were going through because he probably grew up here in the city or somewhere around here. He was more feeling.

Intertwined with students' praise of the class were feelings that Esposito was not like other cops and that he was someone students could speak to with relative ease. But not all students praised the program. Some thought it was boring, that it took away from more important content area classes, and some thought that it was ineffective ("If kids are going to be violent, you can't give them a class and think they're not," one explained). But even some of the criticisms revealed students' desire for intellectual and helpful information about the circumstances that affected them. A white student complained about the program:

> The only thing I didn't like is it was too short . . . because I felt that I didn't learn what I really wanted to learn. He [Officer Esposito] touched bases on a lot of things I wanted to learn, like different laws and what could happen if you do this and why, but I wanted to know more about how getting arrested could affect you for the rest of your life. Because one time I got arrested. I like talking about why certain things happen when you get pulled over because that's what happened to me. I think it should have been longer so we could talk

about more stuff . . . about all the things that happen to us that we can't be sure about.

Challenging common conceptions of DARE that view the program as a stultifying and didactic brainwashing machine, some students, including those who had been arrested or victimized, used the program and Officer Esposito to acquire information that could possibly help them to, if not overcome their predicaments, at least better understand what was happening to them. While Esposito the *police officer* remained for some a threat—complete with the animosities discussed in Chapter 4—for others he was in some ways a powerful symbol of both upward mobility and authority in an economically hurting city. Some students viewed Esposito as they viewed the military (with its presence felt especially on military visiting days when Brandon students were visited by soldier pamphleteers), as a possible means to a job. Several students, all of them boys and primarily working-class (both black and white), asked questions, usually after class, about criteria for becoming a police officer. In addition, Esposito would on occasion talk to the class about the training and the process for signing up for the police academy, one time noting that girls can enter the academy as well.

Less a reflection of the program's benefits than a demonstration of how few opportunities some students had to speak to knowledgeable and caring adults, the program provided some students with chances to discuss issues important to them and to demonstrate their desire for interactions that would be both intellectual and significant to their lives. How this happened could be better understood by looking more closely at a DARE class in action.

VIEWING DARE CLASS

The following is a description of a DARE class that was not atypical. The class took place during the first few weeks of the DARE program and was an example of the role-playing exercises. Officer Esposito considered this class to be one of his most difficult. When I asked him why, he was vague, saying, "They're a little tougher. Kids who have had experiences with this kind of stuff [violence, alcohol, drugs]." In spite of his general enthusiasm and liking for young men and women, Officer Esposito had a negative view of some Brandon High students and preferred the students (especially those who ran track) at North Side High School. But he was also a caring person who seemed willing to engage students in conversation and relished the attention that he received from some. The vignette highlights the students' desire to be engaged in stimulating conversations. It also shows how some of the white boys dominated classes through demonstrations of sexism and male bravado. And, harking back to Chapter 3, it hints at the real consequences for black students of a system that excluded them from full school days through alternative programs and outplacements.

At the beginning of class, Officer Esposito asked a student to hand out the DARE handbooks. One handbook was missing so Esposito borrowed the file cabinet key from the health teacher and left the room to get another. Students quietly talked among themselves while they waited for Esposito to return. The health teacher remained in the class, sitting at her desk in the front corner of the room. There were about 23 students in the classroom—about 8 students were absent. When the officer returned, he gave the handbook to the student who had not gotten one, then stood in front of the class, picked up a piece of chalk, and started by asking the group if they knew what it meant to "reverse the pressure." He rubbed his hands together, looking energetic and anxious for an interesting lesson. "Anybody know—to reverse the pressure?" One white student raised his hand and said, "It's like reverse psychology." Esposito agreed, nodding enthusiastically: "Good, good, good!" He was introducing the first topic of the day: peer pressure. He instructed the students to open to page five of their handbooks. He moved to the other side of the classroom and asked the students, "How can you turn down drugs?" He explained, "You can't just walk up to someone who is smoking and say, 'Hey, what are you doing? Do you know what that stuff does to you?'" A white boy who was sitting next to me chuckled and whispered to his neighbor, "Sure I know what it does. That's why I do it." The neighbor laughed as well, and Esposito looked at the two students as a way of bringing them back into the class lecture.

Esposito explained to the class that there were different ways to turn down drugs. Several students nodded their heads, but most looked at him blankly, seemingly disinterested. Several students in the back became rowdy and began talking freely; one tossed a crumpled ball of paper to another, who batted it with the palm of his hand. Other students who were more reserved doodled on the corners of their handbooks, and one student in the back of the classroom was inconspicuously completing math homework. Esposito turned around and wrote the different kinds of peer pressure on the chalkboard: "friendly," "teasing," "heavy," and "indirect." The class was becoming more restless. Sitting in the center of the room was a group of white boys who continually talked among themselves. The health teacher called to the group, "Okay, now, let's settle down. Settle down!" Esposito tried to quiet the class as well: He told the group, "This material will be on the final test. I think you should pay attention." Several students stopped talking and appeared to pay attention. One student called to the rest, "Shut up, man! I can't hear the *man.*" Esposito told him that he appreciated his efforts but that he did not have to shout.

After making his list on the chalkboard, Esposito asked for a volunteer to help him demonstrate each kind of peer pressure. Again, the person who volunteered was a white student, one of the rowdy boys who sat in the middle area. The boy came to the front of the classroom and Esposito demonstrated "friendly" peer pressure by asking the boy in a nonthreatening way, "Would you like some weed?" The boy told the officer, "Naw, no thanks, man," and Esposito nodded and said, "Sure, no problem," and walked away. He told the boy that he could sit down and told the class, "That's an example of friendly pressure. Nothing too threatening, just somebody asking a question and not pushing you too much." Several students nodded, but most stared at the officer blankly.

Esposito asked for a second volunteer to help him demonstrate "teasing" peer pressure. Again, one of the boys from the center of the room volunteered. He literally jumped to the front of the class. Esposito turned to him and said, "Hey, man, you want to buy some steroids?" The boy began to laugh. He backed away, put his hand over his chest, and said, "No way, man, that gives you breasts." Esposito shook his head and asked him again, "How about some steroids, what, are you afraid?" The boy, who wanted to entertain the class, insisted, "No way, I'll get breasts. Big hairy breasts." Some of the white students sitting in the front of the room laughed. Other students—mostly the girls and African American students—shook their heads, smirked, or did not laugh at the comment. Esposito ended the demonstration. He seemed embarrassed and a bit angry. He turned to the class and said, "Teasing peer pressure is when somebody tries to put you down, but does it subtly, in a joking way, saying something like, 'What, are you afraid?'" The volunteer, who had already taken his seat, whispered to his neighbor, "Damn right I'm afraid of getting breasts." Officer Esposito, who had heard this comment, quickly moved on to the next demonstration.

During the third demonstration, a tall white boy volunteer, who did not seem to be a member of the center group of white students, kept backing away from Esposito toward the door, laughing a bit, uncertain, somewhat embarrassed, partly trying to show off in front of the class. Esposito was trying to demonstrate "heavy" peer pressure by being very forceful. Esposito asked the boy, "Are you ready now?" and the boy nodded. Esposito approached the boy and told him, "Here, have some coke!" Again, the boy backed away, laughing. "Come on, you have to take it seriously," Esposito told him. The student just kept on laughing. Several in the class seemed amused by the display but, again, not all. Esposito told the student to take his seat and explained to the class that "heavy" pressure "is when somebody is almost forcing you to take or drink something. It's not like they are tying you down and forcing it down your throat, but they are being threatening."

For the last demonstration, dealing with indirect pressure, Esposito again asked for a volunteer. This time, a black student, Orlando, who had been rather disruptive throughout class, volunteered. He sat next to the group of white students but, as an African American, was not part of this group. He came to the front of the classroom and faced Officer Esposito. The officer asked him if he was ready, and Orlando nodded. "Okay, this is indirect pressure," Esposito said to the class, then turned to Orlando and asked him, "So how ya doing?" Orlando, who was comic but also serious, gave Esposito "pops"—knocking their fists together—and said, "Okay, man, how ya doing?" Esposito said, "Great, great, man. You want to come to a party?" Orlando told him, "Maybe, what's going down?" "Oh, there'll be music, fun, laughs, you know, the same old . . . weed, smoke, acid, whatever," Officer Esposito told him. One of the boys from the front group chuckled and said to the kid sitting next to him, "Brothers don't do acid." A black student heard this and looked at the white student, and the white student looked at him; then both turned away and directed their attention to the skit.

Orlando shook his head at Esposito, waving his hands: "No, man. I got better things going." Esposito told him, "Hey, it'll be fun. We got everything you could want." Orlando told him, "Naw, I'm being straight with you, I'm not interested." Orlando gave Esposito pops again, and told him, "Catch up with you later, homey." Orlando returned to his seat. A black girl sitting next to him turned to him and said, "You should be an actor." Several in the class, mostly African Americans, applauded. Esposito was pleased with the demonstration as well and explained to the class that "indirect pressure is when someone doesn't come right out and ask you to take drugs but tries to get you involved in something that will lead to drug-taking and drinking."

At this point, an African American girl raised her hand. Esposito called on her and the girl said, "I think the last demonstration was the best." Esposito explained, "Orlando did exactly what you should do—just get out of it by making up an excuse, that way everybody saves face." The girl nodded, "He was cool," she said. Then she said, "I also got a question." "Go ahead," Esposito said, and the girl asked, "Are police dogs trained to bite you?" There had not been any reference to police dogs in the demonstration, so the question seemed a bit off topic, but this did not seem to bother Esposito. He told the girl that police dogs usually had muzzles that prevented them from biting. A few students expressed their concerns in not quite audible mumbles of disapproval. One black student said that the dogs could still bite even with the muzzles on. Another black girl said that she had seen a police dog without a muzzle chasing someone. Esposito did not directly respond to the student's comment; instead, he told a story about an incident when he had responded to a police call, back when he was working the street. There had been a robbery, he explained, and he ended up chasing the thief. Police dogs arrived on the scene and he told the class how he had to stop running or the police dogs might have gone after him. He said that he could have caught the robber because he was a long-distance runner (referring to his track coaching), but if he had not stopped running, the police dogs might not have recognized his uniform and might have attacked him instead of the thief.

At this point, most students became very attentive. Another student asked, "What kinds of dogs are police dogs?" Esposito asked the class if anyone knew, and several said "German Shepard." Esposito nodded and asked the group, "Does anybody know why?" and one student said, "Because they're the dogs that learn the fastest." Esposito agreed and told the class that German Shepards were not vicious, only smart. One student asked, "How do they train the dogs?" and Esposito told her that he was not very sure, but that he had heard that it is very interesting to work with dogs. A student, a white boy who was part of the center group, asked Esposito if any other kinds of dogs were trained. Esposito said, "I'm not sure. I'm not part of the canine squad." Another student asked him, "If you wanted to, could you become part of the canine squad?"

The entire tone of the class had changed during this exchange. The boys in the center were listening intently. Orlando was also interested. He raised his hand and Esposito called on him. He asked, "Do you have to keep your uniform on all the time?" Esposito told him that he was a police officer, and therefore was required to wear his full uniform, though he could perhaps request not to wear it in class. Orlando nodded.

What followed was about 10 minutes of students asking Esposito questions about police work. Esposito answered the questions the best he could, and as always, told short true-life stories to highlight his points. While answering the students' questions, he talked about the differences between being a detective and being an officer—that detectives investigate crimes and that officers did not. He said that New York State was trying to redefine the rank of investigator in order to make it a separate rank of greater authority than officer. One student mentioned that some cops were undercover and that others were "deep under." Esposito said that some police officers in civilian clothes were not undercover, as many think, but were investigating crimes.

Esposito wanted to get back to the curriculum. He asked the class, "What's the best way to deal with indirect pressure?" A student answered, "By just walking away—like Orlando did." He then presented a scenario: "If you were at a party and somebody threw down some weed, and you weren't even smoking, and police came, what would happen to you?" A white student said, "You will be arrested too even if you weren't smoking." Esposito agreed. He asked, "And whose fault is that? Yours or the law?" As in the two other classes where I heard this story told, a black girl responded, "The law." Esposito said, "Yours." The student insisted that if she was not smoking weed then she was not breaking the law. It seemed that Esposito was about to respond, but saw a student with her hand raised, so he called on the student, a white girl, who asked, "Can't they detect drugs in strands of your hair? I heard that they can do that." Esposito said, "Yes. That is true. Through DNA." Then he turned to the class and asked, "Does anybody know anything about that?" Nobody raised a hand, though several remarked that they had heard about DNA in connection with the O.J. Simpson murder trial.

With not much class time remaining, Esposito felt it important to move on quickly. He did not respond to the student who had commented that the law was at fault if a nonsmoker was arrested for attending a party where marijuana was present, avoiding a dispute that had been, in other classes, quite heated. He asked everybody to turn to the next page in their workbooks, but again there was a question. An African American boy asked about the handcuffs dangling from Esposito's belt: "Is that a handcuff key?" referring to a small key next to the handcuffs. With the handbook in his hand, Esposito told him that it was a key, and again was sidetracked from the curriculum. The students became attentive as Esposito explained that his key can open all handcuffs in the city—"that is how police are able to exchange prisoners." He explained, by way of a story: "Imagine," he said, "if I have to arrest somebody in the school—if something really serious happens—and I take the person down to Detective O'Hara's office and Detective O'Hara dismisses me, and I leave. He can take off the handcuffs himself, even though they're mine." Another boy, one from the center of the room, asked Esposito, "Have you ever had to fire your gun?" Esposito told him no, but that he had drawn it on occasion.

Another student asked him if there was a test that police officers had to pass on the firing range. Esposito said that there was, and that he usually did well, but that the last test had not gone well. He had scored 80%, which is the minimum an officer can score. A student asked him what would happen if he failed the test, and Esposito told him that he would have to take training classes. During these questions, most students became attentive. Another student had a question about police cars. He wondered why the police kept changing the types of cars that they used. Esposito asked the students if they knew what kinds of cars the police department used and one said "Fords." Esposito said, "Much of it has to do with dependability. Speed too, but also price."

At this point, two students rose from their desks. Both were African American; one was Orlando. They gathered up their books, slung their book bags onto their shoulders, and started toward the door. Esposito turned to the health teacher and asked, "Is class over?" The health teacher explained that it was not, but that these students had to leave for Central Tech. Neither student seemed particularly happy to leave class. Esposito stopped class until they left and asked Orlando to shut the door behind him. The other students watched them go, and once they were out, Esposito told the rest of the class that they had to move on to page six of their handbooks "or we'll never get through class." Here they discussed different manners of turning down drugs: passive, assertive, and aggressive. The class was rushed. Again, Esposito asked for student volunteers. A Latino boy volunteered and gave Esposito a bit of a hard time. Esposito asked the boy to offer him crack. The boy asked the officer, "You want some crack, man?" Esposito told the boy—demonstrating "passive means" of turning down drugs—"No, no. Don't you remember our DARE class, what they taught us?" The boy said, "Forget about that. You can read that stuff in *Time* magazine."

Esposito quickly moved on to the next demonstration. Again, he asked for a volunteer. The atmosphere of the class had changed again, returning to a blend of disinterest and rowdiness. For the second demonstration, one of the white boys from the center of the room volunteered. On cue, he asked Esposito if he wanted some beer and Esposito, demonstrating the "aggressive method," stood on his toes and shouted, "What are you, crazy? Get away from me!" Unexpectedly, the student lunged forward and shouted back at Esposito, "What, are YOU crazy!" Some of the students laughed, but again, others did not seem pleased with this student's way of showing off. The student took a low bow for the class and swaggered back to his seat.

When it was time for the last demonstration, the health teacher, Officer Esposito, and several students insisted that a girl should volunteer. "Come on, girls," the health teacher called, "let's see one of you at the front of the room." But the girls refused to participate. The boy who had made the comment about steroids giving him breasts stood up for the final demonstration. He came to the front of the room, but the bell rang before he and Esposito could begin the skit. The boy returned to his desk, grabbed his books, and followed the crowd out of the classroom, while Esposito reminded them to leave their handbooks on their desks so that he could collect them.

BEING SMART

While one might consider the students' questioning of Esposito examples of their "being smart" in a way that demonstrated their interest and intelligence, others might say that their questions were another kind of "smart," one that displayed their sarcasm and disrespect for authority (as in "smart-aleck"). Because of his mixed feelings for Brandon High students, and his own defensiveness as a rather proud police officer, Esposito considered the students' questions somewhere in the middle of these two kinds of smart. The classes that Esposito determined to be the most difficult were the ones containing students who asked the most analytical questions, such as the class just described. At the same time, he also answered most of the students' questions, seemed to enjoy the attention and enthusiasm that came from them, and on occasion admitted that they asked good questions.

How students interacted with the police officer, and the types of questions they asked, said something about students' experiences in the city and their concerns about violence. In general, mostly white and middle-class students showed interest in police procedures that were not part of their experiences and were steeped in technology and training, regarding drug testing, DNA, and the canine squad, for example. They did not often challenge the honesty and integrity of the police. They were not smart in the sarcastic sense. In general, being smart for these kids meant acquiring chunks of knowledge that would be of interest to those who saw themselves pursuing professional lives and lifestyles.

On the other hand, African American and poor students, who experienced what most white and middle-upper-class people know only as national headlines about yet another case of police brutality, honed in on police injustices. Their focus was not on the distant and invisible, but on the ground-level and daily experiences of life in the ghetto. Being smart for African American and poor students meant a talk about social injustice colored with challenges and accusations aimed at city power structures, police, and prejudices. All students expressed their interests and perspectives in a way that was filtered through their own experiences and upbringings. In the case of poor black students, these expressions were channeled through the culture and injustices of city streets.

African American girls were often the most challenging and analytical. In the eyes of other students, they were loud, and in Esposito's mind, they were anti-cop. They were the type of girls who would be classified by school staff as "bad sista" types. As Fordham (1993) and Cousins (1999, p. 307) explained, being black, female, and loud is a mix that "complicates social class categories" because girls invert gender roles by making use of social-class expectations of assertiveness and a direct ("no beating around the bush") kind of combativeness associated with working-class boys. It was not only their race and gender at work here, but also their socioeconomic class, since many middle-class black girls seemed as distant from these other more assertive girls as did the middle-class boys in the room.

In one class, for example, an African American girl whose parents were middle-class professionals wanted to know if people really got shot for dealing drugs, and when several students ridiculed her (including several black girls), she rephrased her question, saying, "I meant, do they actually get shot here, in this city?" which caused further ridicule. Not only is this an example of ridicule that students must put up with, but it also typifies how interpretations of violence are class-situated and reflective of experiences in neighborhoods. There was nothing accusatory or threatening about the girl's question, nothing that put Officer Esposito on the spot. But the questions put forth by the "loud black girls" were a different story.

The following vignette of a DARE class was typical of the way some African American girls challenged white and middle- and upper-class interpretations of violence. These kinds of interactions became more prevalent during the last days of the DARE program.

After handing out the workbooks for class, Officer Esposito went to the blackboard and wrote:

rules—to promote learning

laws—to promote human health and safety

He turned, faced the students, and told them, "In school there are laws and rules to follow—we all know this." He then asked the class if there were things that a student can do outside but not inside of school. The class seemed disinterested and quiet, so Officer Esposito offered his own answer: "What about wearing a hat and a Walkman? You can do that outside of school but not inside." A black girl raised her hand. Esposito called on her and she said, "You can't be wearing a hat and Walkman in the street if you're a black male." Officer Esposito asked her, "What do you mean?" The girl said, "It's about color." There was silence in the class for a moment. Then another black girl added, to back up the first, "You can't be wearing certain things if you're a certain type." "What type?" Esposito asked. And the girl, guffawing, said, "Black type, *man*." A Latino boy said, "And you can't be wearing no *hoody* either," reminding me of officers' references to "hood rats." Then another black girl said, "And if you're driving around in a nice car, they'll find something wrong so they can pull you over and hassle you." Suddenly the class seemed energized, students staring at Officer Esposito, waiting to see how he would react.

Another black girl asked, "Ain't it true that a man police can't search a girl and a girl cop can't check a boy—that that can be sexual harassment?" Esposito seemed more comfortable with this type of question than the previous ones. He relaxed a bit and explained that for most cases this was true—that a male cop had to call a female cop to the scene to body-search a girl. But he remarked that it all depended on the circumstances. A male cop could check the pockets and bag of a girl. Also, if there was a strong reason to believe that the girl was carrying a weapon, the male cop could body-search the girl. The African American girl who had first challenged Esposito about the Walkman and hat issue asked, "Why can cops just search people without any reason?" Esposito told her that police officers needed "probable cause" to search individuals.

The girl was dissatisfied with his answer and highlighted her point with the following story: She was coming home from her grandmother's house at night and saw a cop search some friends. She was with her cousins and the cops came up and started searching them for apparently no reason. One of her cousins had a pipe ("for protection"), and the cops just threw it on a lawn and left after searching them. She said, "The cop saw my friend pick up the pipe but didn't do anything. They just wanted to hassle us." Esposito explained that her friend had a pipe, which is a weapon. But the girl wanted to know, "How come he didn't arrest him, then, if it's a weapon?" Esposito responded by deflecting attention away from the specific circumstances and tried to justify the actions of the officers: "You don't know if maybe a neighbor had called the police and that's why the police came. That's the problem so often, people see police officers questioning people and they think that they are just randomly picking on people when it fact maybe somebody had called the police and complained about someone." This explanation did not satisfy the girl. She shook her head and mumbled to her neighbor, "It makes no sense."

Further delving into the nature of law and justice, another African American girl asked, "Can people get arrested for saying something that isn't true?" Esposito explained that they could, that they could be charged with "falsely reporting an incident." The first girl asked, "If cops check you and you have some money, can they take it away?" A girl and boy, both of whom were black, nodded their heads knowingly. The boy said, "That happens all the time." Esposito said, "They have badge numbers and names. I am on your side if police officers are breaking the law. That is police corruption." The girl said that that happened to her friend, the cops took his money. The African American boy said that that had happened to him and his friend—that they had to go downtown to claim their money. The first girl said, "It all depends what color you are." Esposito said, "There is no reason for people to search other people unless there is a reason." The girl said, "They're black. That's the reason."

Officer Esposito tried to return to the curriculum, regarding the differences between rules and laws, but the African American girls in the class, who also wanted to discuss rules and laws, wanted to do so in a way that made sense to them. They wanted to talk in a way that reflected their own experiences and enabled them to assert their own authority on the matter, regardless of how "inappropriate" their assertions may seem to middle-class sensibilities. In other classes, the dynamics were similar. In one class, Esposito told a story about a kid who tried to outrun the police because he was high on weed. In response, an African American girl said, "Maybe it wasn't the weed. Maybe he was scared of the cops." The following vignette points out a similar dynamic:

In one class, a white student wanted to know if it was illegal to go to a party if there were drugs present. Esposito told the boy, and announced to the class, that people should not go to parties that may involve drugs or alcohol. A black girl said, "It's okay to go to that party." Esposito disagreed and told her, "You'd probably end up taking something." The girl insisted, "I wouldn't. I've got a will of my own."

Esposito continued to disagree with her, saying, "It's not a good thing. If you're at a party like that, you are inviting trouble." The girl said, "I ain't that gullible." She insisted that she would go to court to fight any charges caused by an arrest for only being at a party where drugs were present. Officer Esposito told her, "That's expensive." The girl said, "I don't care," and explained how she would fight to the very end and spend every penny she had. Esposito said, "Every time you walk in a door of a party like that, you are taking a risk. Do you know if you do get arrested, the cops are not picking on you?" The girl said, "I don't smoke. They will be picking on me." Esposito disagreed, and said, "In a party situation, who knows what will happen?" The girl sat up in her seat and said, sarcastically, "Okay, okay, I won't go to any more parties" and laughed to her neighbor.

Perhaps feeling safer than the black guys in the class—who may have learned not to challenge the police—the black girls aimed their comments at the core issues of racial politics, police conduct, and community tensions. Unlike girls in studies that have rightly focused on female students who participate in their own invisibility in school by remaining silent and "suffering quietly" (Steet, 1998, p. 113), working-class African American girls at Brandon High who appropriated male prerogatives to use "in your face" tactics to defend and assert were another side of the student invisibility debate. Unlike traditional "invisible child" students, these girls were not victims of a silenced dialogue, per se; rather they were perceived as loud and inappropriate, and therefore dismissed. If they did participate in their own invisibility, they did so not through silence but through loud persistent claims that were, nevertheless, not heard.

THE BENEFITS OF DARE

Most students seemed to benefit from the DARE program to some extent. In general, they benefited by having what was for many students an interesting class that enabled them to speak to a new face in the school about issues that were for some more pressing than those usually discussed in the traditional content area classes. Even if schools may never be ready or willing to address the most controversial of students' questions, they should be, at the very least, willing and ready to incorporate into classes the level of intellectual engagement that students sought at Brandon High through their questioning and curiosity. Ultimately, the effects of the program depend on many factors, including the talents of individual DARE teachers, the willingness of teachers to take seriously the critical realities of students' lives, and the mentalities and predicaments of particular students.

Even the role of the health teacher has an effect on DARE classes. In one class, for example, a health teacher who had remained in the room during DARE drastically shifted the tone of the class, which had been about nonviolence. In this instance, a student brought up the issue of self-defense, a topic that was discussed in most of the classes I observed, though it was not part of the DARE curriculum. He asked, "If a thief broke into somebody's house, could the person living in the house shoot him?" Officer Esposito tried to explain that it all depended on the circumstances. Suddenly, the health teacher said, nearly rising from her desk, "If they're breaking into your house, you shoot them!" It was a sudden outburst from somebody who had yet to speak in any DARE class—a teacher who usually corrected papers while Esposito taught. The outburst may have been triggered by a 1997 incident involving a Brandon High social studies teacher who had been tied up and stabbed by intruders in his house. This was a crime that was widely reported in the city newspaper and was for many weeks the talk of the school. Regardless of the cause of the outburst, some of the students agreed with the teacher's assessment with nods of the head and mumbled phrases: "you bet," "blow 'em away," "got to protect yourself."

In spite of the groundswell against him, Esposito held his ground and explained to the class that an individual needed "just cause" in this case. But the health teacher insisted, nearly shouting, "You shoot them! You have to shoot them!" Before Esposito could respond or make sense of this disruption, the teacher wanted to know, "How come they protect criminals so much?" The teacher seemed to want to rally students to her side, and it caused the class to become nearly uncontrollable. One white student pumped his arm in the air as if cheering on a football team; others shouted their agreement with the teacher; one African American student pointed two fingers at his neighbor's head and demonstrated how he would blow his brains out. Esposito said very clearly over the loudness of the classroom, "It's not always the best thing to shoot someone." He mentioned the Brandon High teacher who had been stabbed and explained that if the teacher had resisted, the criminals might have killed him. The class was getting quieter now, but remained passionate. Esposito told them, disagreeing with the health teacher, "Excessive force is not good." But it did not seem that anybody was listening to him.

Regardless of one's opinions regarding the thief scenario and whether the students had been (or should have been) swayed by the health teacher, the fact remains that the class, through the teacher's prodding, rallied around the simplistic rule that you shoot first and ask questions later. Officer Esposito's more balanced view—that excessive force is not good and that individuals needed to consider circumstances—was drowned out as students created a ruckus around the health teacher's "take no prisoners" mentality.

This is but one example of the difficultly of determining the effectiveness of DARE. Classes are too dynamic and unpredictable to measure the effectiveness of an entire program. Even a good program may be undermined by any number of circumstances in the classroom, such as a poor DARE teacher or a highly influential health teacher with a negative attitude; likewise, a poor program may be salvaged by a terrific teacher or by extremely motivated students.

Also significant about DARE at Brandon High was the fact that some students were excluded from a portion of the program by school policies, such as their placement in Central Tech and adult education. DARE classes that were held in the afternoon were not attended by students who had early dismissal. This must also be considered when evaluating effectiveness. As we saw in Chapter 3, students who were given outplacements were often those who had had the most experience with violence and associated problems of poverty, family breakdown, substance abuse, and gangs. If DARE is, in fact, effective in helping students to avoid violence, then it would be foolish to exclude these students from taking it. Also, when programs are evaluated, one must wonder if these students are involved in the studies.

POWER, OWNERSHIP, AND DARE

In many ways, students were using the DARE class to assert power—the power to tell about their lives, the power to sway people, the power to challenge, and in some cases, the power to harass. To start with these interactions and this student energy may be more beneficial than using the essentially behaviorist curriculum currently in place. But a problem persists: To take seriously this energy, teachers must not only veer away from the standard curriculum and the policies that support DARE, but also align themselves with those who challenge power structures in schools and neighborhoods. To start, DARE officers must take seriously student claims of police harassment and racism—quite a task, to say the least. In addition, officers must acknowledge how white, heterosexual, and middle-class power is used in the classroom as a form of violence—a way of putting down people, of harassing, of drowning out the input of those whose life experiences differ from the mainstream.

In two classrooms, groups of white boys dominated discussions almost daily and their comments were sometimes sexist, racist, and homophobic. They attempted to turn attention to themselves by wresting focus away from the topics raised by African American students, especially the black girls. Certainly, broader patterns of harassment in the school continued through DARE classes. Like the male students described by Willis (1977) and Foley (1990), these Brandon boys used power endowed on them by virtue of their maleness and a rakish sense of humor to challenge, not in this case the school, but interpretations of violence put forth by students unlike themselves. With bawdy comments and maliciousness, they attempted to sanitize violence and preserve their conceptions of crime, race, and the police as essentially black-and-white issues having to do with mostly good police versus mostly bad poor black kids. For these white middle-class students, to question the legitimacy of drug laws and the honesty of police officers complicated issues of violence and challenged white middle-class worldviews.

Naturally, how the DARE program is taught depends in large part on the police officer teaching the class. To what degree is he or she willing to challenge and be challenged by students, veer from the curriculum, and have high expectations and respect for all students? Essentially, police officers must make persistent efforts to defy comments and discussions that decontextualize violence and substance abuse. They must intervene when students are harassing one another in ways that are vicious and steeped in prejudice. What Roman (1993, pp. 82–84) called a pedagogy that would be a "socially transformative practice of critical realism" would require that DARE officers take on the highly charged politics that would accompany any "critically realistic" discussion about drugs, alcohol, and violence in society. Responding to criticism of the program, in early 2001 the developers of DARE decided that they would revise the curriculum to include more role-playing and problem-solving activities for students. While the incorporation of these activities seems like a commendable improvement, such alterations will not change the basic, behaviorist curriculum of the DARE program. What is needed is a pedagogy that takes as its starting point the lives of students who are caught up in violence and that takes seriously the perspectives of young people, even when they are criticizing adults. This would require that DARE officers follow the lead of some students who remark loudly and clearly that discussions about violence must also entail conversations about power, corruption, race, patronage, prejudice, city politics, and the economic and social structures of policing and punishment in the United States.

CHAPTER 7

Public Policy, Popular Discourse, and Education Reform

The high school is a unique institution—a place where police officers, youth, teachers, social workers, administrators, counselors, parents, psychologists, and others come together, not always without strife, for the education of teenagers. At Brandon High, the hallways, classrooms, cafeteria, gym, bathrooms, and parking lot were intense and energetic with the interactions of different groups of students, teachers, and others who created the institution. In the day-to-day workings of the school, sometimes violence was a part of the rhythm. At times—when there were fights, when Detective O'Hara got involved to arrest a student, when worries grew feverish from a suicide threat or a shooting the night before—the school would be awash with feelings of tension, fear, concern, unknowing, and danger.

At other times—when walking in the basement of the school or during mellow days when students quietly moved to their four block periods and sat calmly behind the doors of their classrooms—the school could almost seem lulled into a solemn and even lonely place, like being in an empty office building. Days would be rather uneventful, even boring. Detective O'Hara would have time to catch up on paperwork and I would stop in to visit him in his office and he would nod to his quiet walkie-talkie sitting on his filing cabinet and tell me "no news is good news." The counselors would take time to catch up on scheduling duties, and the assistant principals and the principal would seem less visible. On these days, worries about violence were the extent of the problem.

Regardless of the particular mood of the school at the time, whether intense or solemn, there was always, as one assistant principal explained, a subtle "red-alert feeling" in the air. Those in the school referred to this feeling in their offhand remarks about the potential of violence: "Well, you never know," and "There's never a dull moment." Even during the quietest of days, a close look under the still veneer revealed administrators meeting with parents about particular students who were having troubles with police, fighting, bad behavior, or rumors regarding gangs or drugs. There was hardly a morning when a student did not get suspended or recommended for peer mediation. Each week students came before the screening committee and gang tensions were always a part of some students' days. Even the quietness of some afternoons could not cancel out these realities.

School violence was part of a low-level and persistent worry that was expressed in unfortunate ways, especially in disciplinary policy and in behaviors that deflected attention from education and fueled paranoias. The school spent much daily energy on violence prevention and intervention not only with its DARE classes, but also with committee meetings, drills, and workshops run by the police department and the C-Pep psychiatric ward. But while efforts at violence prevention were commendable, sometimes worries overtook the school. This, of course, was reflective of a school year that brought with it some of the first news of school massacres. But the reaction is one that has continued and at times preceded the worst of the school shootings, and exists in other schools in other states (McQuillan, 1998; Noguera, 1995; Ward, 1995).

Violence in schools is one formation of a larger street, sexual, racial, and political violence in the United States. At Brandon High it involved actions that were expressed through a context made up of urban poverty, cultural prejudice and misunderstandings, emotion and fear, policy and discipline, and historical relationships involving police officers, youth, and the criminal justice system. School violence is not just about "out-of-control kids" or "dangerous cops" or "oppressive schools." It also is part of a political establishment that has historically condoned violence and the mass proliferation of weapons, of a society that naturalizes violence for youth but does not listen to them, of individuals who have dealt poorly with prejudice and conflicts, and of policies that aim to punish those with problems.

LINKING THEORY AND PRACTICE

As a member of a state advisory committee on school violence, I attended a meeting in 1999 in Connecticut during which the discussion about school violence turned to prevention strategies. While each member of the committee—made up of state and police representatives, directors of social services, city school district employees, and other educators—gave suggestions about prevention, I kept wanting to know, "What violence are we talking about?" Is one person talking about white students spraying hallways and playgrounds with bullets while another is referring to sexual harassment? Is one group talking about tensions and attacks involving mostly African

American and Latino gangs while another is talking about the bullying of short, quiet, fat, disabled, or other types of outcast students? Is one concerned about suicide while another is talking about hallway and cafeteria fights brought on by rumors, sexual relations, and revenge? Or are some talking about acts of racism, sexism, and other prejudices, while another group is focusing on fights over food or money?

Sometimes we look for solutions to social problems without agreeing on what the problem really is. Identifying the problem is important because each form of school violence deserves a different kind of attention, and by extension a different type of prevention, reform, or intervention strategy. A prevention effort to address issues associated with fights between African American and Latino girls requires an approach very different from that needed to address high suicide rates among white boys. While there are similar issues involved, in the first case we need to be understanding about the lives and circumstances of minority girls. These circumstances can include greater competition for men due in part to high rates of incarceration among minority males, gender roles that can be oppressive and demeaning, circumstances involving babies and absentee fathers, abuse by men and sometimes by other females. In the second case, we must attend to issues regarding hopelessness and a kind of quiet desperation especially among white boys but among other groups as well. If we are talking about gangs, we must take into account the role that neighborhoods play and the economics of drug selling and weapon dealing, lack of meaningful employment, peer pressure, and the gangster mentality. These are different problems with different solutions.

Policy must reflect the physical, systemic, hidden, and emotional realities of school violence in all of its forms, instead of just focusing on lethal violence and allocating money for prevention and liaisons that intend to change the behaviors of students without changing the environments in which they live and become educated. Federal policy, followed up with grants, must also develop a means to restructure schools in order to promote equity, respect, and inclusiveness, rather than just add on to semi-faulty systems. Violence occurs within a context and sometimes the context adds to the problem, or makes violence more likely to happen. In a building that can be alienating, where people are crowded in for long hours each day, where there are tensions for multiple reasons, where there is an unbreakable link between the school and community problems and little time for people to talk freely and to meet in friendly ways, the context pumps up the alienating experiences, tensions, and power struggles that often turn violent.

In order to prevent violence, individuals must recognize how history, economics, and culture are often the driving forces behind violent incidents.

In their prevention work, they must be able to link structural issues of policy, city politics, and inequality to concerns involving behavior, race, gender, gangs, and poverty. We also need to listen to young people, to appreciate their insights as they describe their conflicts and what is needed (from both adults and youth) to solve the problem. A means of reform would have to be as broad as the parameters of violence itself. In short, a reform effort must cover a lot of conflict-worn ground. The strategies I suggest are based on the following five premises discussed in this book:

1. Violence is the result of an intersection between systemic problems associated with social and economic inequities in society and a dynamic youth culture that treats violence as an appropriate reaction to conflict.
2. Schools exacerbate inequities in society, including those that act as sources of violence, by reproducing in the school the alienation and segregation that characterize many students' lives.
3. Most violence-prevention efforts focus on students as the locus of the problem, viewing student behavior as that which needs to be "fixed" through various forms of threats, punishments, and behavior modifications.
4. "Community policing" efforts are doomed to failure when relationships between police and minority youth are antagonistic, even hateful, fueling traditional policing based on arresting, not helping.
5. The life experiences and insights of young people who are the victims and perpetrators of most violence are not often recognized in violence prevention programs and policies.

In what follows, I give an overview of attainable reforms needed in schools to address the issues identified in the five premises. A common thread running through the reforms is the need for a collaborative and long-term effort to improve the lives of young people with inclusive, fair, and academically challenging public schools.

EDUCATION REFORM IN SHORT

The five reform strategies that I cover here loosely match the five premises listed above.

• *Reform 1:* School and community liaisons must be developed among social service organizations and activists, students, caring school staff, parents, and police officers. These liaisons must aim to address violence in a manner that empowers students not only to alter their behaviors, but also to force changes in their communities through protest, organizing, and policy reform. Top-down methods of violence prevention must be replaced with social actions that hold middle-class society accountable for the violence caused through its own policies and practices that sustain segregation, poverty, and power imbalances in schools and communities. Cities have lost much political clout, but federal money does exist, and there are community facilities and resources, to develop working partnerships that can press change through voting drives, petitioning, and media advocacy. Schools should be used as community meeting places where problems of violence are solved not just by professionals, but also by students, concerned community members, and parents. Federal money should facilitate the hiring of community organizers and neighborhood revitalization programs that take into account the wants of residents.

• *Reform 2:* All exclusionary practices in schools must be eliminated. Various kinds of outplacements are a means of placing students away from those who are valued in the school. This is a form of tracking—of "subtracking," really. Schools must be inclusive and have the resources and staff to make inclusive education possible. For example, zero tolerance must be replaced with more caring practices that involve students in the school, not force them out. School staff must take responsibility for providing what all students need: support, high academic expectations, and contacts with individuals that enable success. In integrated and heterogenous classrooms, high expectations should be the norm with extra staff and team-teaching providing extra help for those students needing it. Tutoring and mentoring programs that are well run and well supported must be made available and convenient for all students and must be an alternative to suspension and expulsion. Student groups, including those of a controversial nature, that would promote justice, caring, and support for each other should be urged to use the school to meet and discuss issues important to them.

• *Reform 3:* Violence-prevention programs and strategies, including peer mediation, character education, DARE, and behavior modification, must move beyond behaviorist notions of delinquency. Peer mediation programs must be made up of students and staff who work long-term with students to prevent violence, sponsor violence-reduction meetings, and negotiate with administrators about discipline policy. Violence-prevention and conflict resolution efforts should be an ongoing process of trust and advocacy between youth and adults, a concerted effort that gains the support of most people involved. Students need to be educated about their emotions, impulses, and actions. Likewise, school staff must recognize and be taught through in-service or professional development that forms of sexual harassment and bullying are in fact violent. They must know how to address the problem in a fair and just way. Before outright violence occurs, school staff must intervene and talk to students when there is a brimming conflict (and not just call security). Staff need time during the day to get to know students. It should be part of all teacher education programs that prospective teachers be taught to recognize forms of violence, to know how to deal with conflicts, and to always consider the integrity of students of utmost importance.

  • *Reform 4:* Relationships between police officers and youth must be improved. Community policing efforts are a sham when many youth dislike police and when many officers hold racist attitudes or a general dislike for young people. Police training, especially for school police officers, must include more than enforcement methods; it must include expectations that police *protect* youth—not attack them. All those charged with the duty of school security must understand ways of interacting with young people in respectful ways. School officers should regularly meet with groups of students and parents to discuss issues of violence, discipline, and security. Community residents, including youth, must also participate in determining how school police conduct their jobs, which could be best done if a civic association were to oversee policing in schools and have a strong say in the hiring of security personnel. Behaviorist and rational-choice theories of violence must be replaced with a view that sees youth as individuals who are not only victimizers, but also victimized, as well as capable of contributing to efforts to improve the school. If school security cannot advocate for students it should be abolished.

  • *Reform 5:* The perspectives of poor and minority youth must be considered when schools set out to develop violence-prevention programs. Many youth see violence in the actions of adults, in bullying and harassment, and in a school system that alienates those who are labeled. And these realities must be addressed in a way that recognizes the validity of what students say and their capacity to solve the problem. There may be no better person to mediate fights than one who has been in fights. James Vigil (1999) made the point that gang interventions are most productive when gang members take part in the prevention efforts. Teacher education, professional development, and in-service work should impress on educators the importance of working with young people to create a learning experience that would be challenging, uplifting, and worth each kid's time and effort. This can be done only with the students' help and cooperation. Site-based management of schools must become institutionalized and powerful enough so that students, parents, and teachers have greater impact on the running of the school—and it must not be permitted that students' voices are drowned out by the more experienced parents and teachers. A governance committee made up of students that had opportunities to meet regularly with the school board and administrators would aid in students' access to policy and decision-making processes.

There is little reason why students should behave if adults are creating institutions for them that the adults themselves do not like. Both students and staff must be happy in school. This is the only way to ensure that all people take part in the creation of a peaceful building where inspiration and uplifting challenges are always a part of all educational experiences. But part of the problem is that teachers, administrators, counselors, social workers, and other staff are burnt-out and stressed. Sometimes they do not empathize with students, partly because they are given truly difficult (if not impossible) jobs, partly because they are extremely busy, and also because professionalism often sets up adults' and kids' interests as oppositional (Smith, 1996). To the professional mind, young people are subjects to be trained and molded in the likeness of the professionals themselves, not according to what the students want for themselves. When students fail to impress, or become an embarrassment, in triage fashion the school begins to favor those who are doing fine. The rest fall by the wayside.

Adding a program to a school system that alienates students will not prevent violence—it just makes for another program in an unjust school. Telling students who live in ghettos to "just straighten out" or to "get their act together" underestimates the dire effects of poverty on their lives. Students are too often the targets of reform policies—and in many instances they continue to bear the brunt of adults' frustrations with social problems—even when adults are attempting to solve *their* problems for *their* own good. Adults too must be held accountable for the state of our schools and communities. All practices that alienate students, reproduce inequities, and treat students as criminals for misbehaving must be eliminated in favor of practical and ongoing moves to create schools where the power imbalances that exist in society are not reproduced, but are replaced with supportive relationships and equitable treatment for all students. This is what students—what all of us—need in order to succeed.

THE SCHOOL AND THE CITY REVISITED

School violence is more than urban blight, but that there exists more school violence in urban areas than elsewhere is generally true (NCES, 1998; Petersen et al., 1998; Pinderhughes, 1997; Sampson, 1997). School violence in cities is a kind of subset of urban violence, and may have more to do with problems associated with street violence in ghettos than with the causes of violence in suburban schools. As Nancy Guerra (1997, p. 298) noted, "Conducting preventive interventions in the inner city poses challenges not encountered in more privileged environments" and, therefore, prevention strategies must consider how violence in schools is exacerbated by broader urban problems. These broader problems include inadequate prenatal and health care, high incidence of abuse, birth traumas, poverty, transience, lack of adult supervision, poor schools and communities, entrenched gangs, and the selling and use of drugs and weapons. Faced with such deprivations and problems, youth do not just internalize antisocial behavior; they experience each day the blocked opportunities, the forces that keep them down, and the real pressures that these problems cause.

At Brandon High, incidents of fighting and gang violence were the terrain of mostly poor, black, and Latino students—those on the "prison track." These were not students with bright prospects for the future—in some cases they did not have a future. The (mostly) intraracial violence associated with drugs, gangs, money, turf, and respect will continue in schools as long as it continues in neighborhoods. And it will continue in neighborhoods as long as cities continue to be decimated by economic neglect and loss of political power. Politicians who seem willing to support "safe school programs" must shift their focus to support ongoing acts to reinvest in neighborhoods—to hold landlords, businesses, and homeowners accountable for the state of their properties; to improve public works; to increase neighborhood policing with caring officers; and to solve school funding inequities caused by property tax financing (as well as patronage and mismanagement of funds). To address violence in urban schools without addressing violence and inequities in the city, to use Jean Anyon's (1997, p. 168) phrase, "is like trying to clean the air on one side of a screen door."

In her study of Newark, New Jersey, a city in some ways similar to Brandon city, Anyon (1997) concluded:

> Unfortunately, educational "small victories" such as the restructuring of a school or the introduction of a new classroom pedagogical technique, no matter how satisfying to the individuals involved, without a long-range strategy to eradicate underlying causes of poverty and racial isolation, cannot add up to large victories in our inner cities with effects that are sustainable over time. (p. 165)

The sustainability of violence prevention depends on the degree to which it connects with the environmental, racial, and economic bearings of society. Poverty in cities that leads to violence is part of many problems including patronage and corruption, highway expansion and improved travel, relocation and immigration, globalization and housing patterns, poor policy and prejudice. This history of "urban blight" that begins with the industrial revolution and continues today has led to a unique situation in cities. It is a situation with an interconnected history involving youth, institutionalization, professionalism, violence, police departments, gangs, and schools' closer links with the criminal justice system.

School policy cannot ignore what people at Brandon High call the blurring lines between "school problems" and "neighborhood problems." Any violence-prevention strategy must be a part of students' neighborhoods and experiences, since, as most school staff know, violence in schools and that in neighborhoods are already linked. Violence prevention does not mean just changing people's behaviors, though that is a part of it. It also means changing the squalor and hopelessness that characterize the places where young people live and sometimes, tragically, die.

SCHOOL RESTRUCTURING FOR A JUST ENVIRONMENT

The implementation of strategies to improve city economics, and to alleviate poverty and racial segregation, will not by itself prevent school violence. In addition, schools must be committed to creating just environments. As Nel Noddings (1996, p. 186) noted in her observations of students, "Kids seem able to survive material poverty, and many can ignore much of the violence in the media—or, at least, keep its effects to a minimum—if they have continuing relationships with adults who obviously care about them." Too often, in the rush to improve test scores and to "cover the curriculum," in the panic to keep the school orderly, amid the tensions of teaching and conducting the administrative duties in a school, many adults forget that students need to feel supported and have opportunities to support others.

In order for schools to develop relationships that would lead to more peaceful buildings, those in the education profession must be committed to changing aspects of schools that have put mostly minority males at the center of a "school-police-justice system" triad. This must be done while setting in place organizational changes (smaller classes, inclusive education, nonexclusionary discipline policy) that would enable teachers and administrators to better know and work with students (Noddings, 1992; Oakes, 1995; Ward, 1995). Too often, schools implement reforms that are meant to improve school environments and relationships, but the primary purpose of the reform gets lost in the implementation of it.

At Brandon High, many classrooms had only about 15 students in them, but the small classes were the result of a high dropout rate and not of any kind of reform. They represented failure, not good policy. How schools implement reform, the reason they do it, and what must be done away with in the process are as important as the reform itself. While many studies, including the Safe School Study and Senator Bayh's report of the 1970s, have indicated that a firm and consistent form of discipline is important to the development of peaceful schools, too often "firm and consistent" is interpreted to mean "severe."

While firm, fair, and consistent leadership and discipline accompany schools with few problems of violence, arbitrary leadership and severe disciplinary actions characterize schools with high levels of aggression (Goldstein, 1994, p. 37). When students are treated unjustly, they will react as most adults will: They will fight back. In their study of school violence, Gary Gottfredson and Denise Gottfredson (1985) described the detrimental effects of expulsion and suspension in a way that made much sense for what was going on at Brandon High, especially in regard to their screening committee and policing efforts:

> School disorder tends to be greatest in schools serving communities characterized by social disorganization and largely minority populations; therefore, many of the students removed from school by such policies would tend to be minority youth and youths from disorganized neighborhoods. The likely effect of such policies would be to maintain or exacerbate inequality in the educational attainment of minority groups and the perpetuation of social disorganization in communities. (p. 188)

Expulsion and suspension send troubled students back to communities where they are in greater contact with those who have also been expelled or who have dropped out of school. They put kids in the company of those who are young, bored, and not working. Expulsion does not help expelled students; it does not teach them a lesson. Similar to what occurs in prisons, it reintroduces young people to an environment adults would rather keep them away from. Nor does a school reap substantial advantages from expulsion. While some staff (and students) will argue that one less violent student in school means at least one less violent incident, this is an example of what Anyon (1997) means by a "small victory." These students inevitably return to school and do so with less respect and, in some cases, a more combative attitude. Students know when schools do not want them—and expulsion is a very pronounced message of this. The violence that students do is real, and it might be any person's initial response to want to just get rid of a violent kid. But while perhaps an understandable reaction, this response does not solve the problem.

There were simple daily incidents at Brandon High that could speak volumes about the importance of adult support and care for students. Success stories were the other side of school violence, for they hinted at what works in maintaining peace and positiveness in a building. Toward the end of the winter in 1998, I was in the guidance suite when an ex-Brandon student came to visit his old counselor, Ms. Evers. Ben had pulled through Brandon High, in the words of the counselor, "by the skin of his teeth," and had a way of talking, and an accent, that was distinctly urban—a southern sound with a northeastern back-beat that he punctuated with his hands. His two front teeth set in gold harked back to a time of yesterday's gang fashions. Ben had come to thank Ms. Evers for her help getting him into the city community college when he was a senior, 2 years before. He now had plans to go to Florida for school to study oceanography and talked about these ambitions with great enthusiasm and pride.

Ben brought along his younger cousin, who had been placed in the afternoon school program, and wanted to know if the counselor could do anything about this. His management of the situation was professional, friendly, and to the point. Ms. Evers seemed truly pleased to see Ben and told me later that she had "taken him under her wing" while he was in school: "He wasn't really a bad kid, but a kid who had some real problems." The counselor told Ben that she would see to it that his cousin had another screening committee meeting to consider him for day school but that she could not guarantee anything. Ben urged her to sign him up for a screening immediately, "so none of us forget," and asked if he could come to the screening. Ms. Evers agreed that he could and scheduled the screening for the following week. Ben shook the counselor's hand, the counselor gave Ben a quick hug and wished him luck. Then Ben shook my hand and promptly left the office, offering up multiple good-byes and thanks.

Ben was a student who had been given a chance at Brandon High; he was taken under somebody's wing. No doubt, he was also a kid who had caused trouble, who had fought, and who might have been suspended or expelled. But he had been liked by his counselor—and perhaps others. In addition, he had learned how to maneuver and charm his way through a school bureaucracy. He was now using his abilities not only to advance himself, but also to help a cousin. How much good the screening committee meeting will do for Ben's cousin is questionable (I was unable to attend). But with Ben behind him, the cousin will no doubt have a better chance at success than if he were to do it alone. Ben, and now Ben's cousin, had a support that is missing from the lives of too many adolescents. Though schools cannot be the families of young people, they can support those whose families have all but given up on them.

Students who act violently are violent at the same time that they are confused, or stuck in the middle of a serious dilemma, or angry, or fed up, or feeling lost in their lives. These are students who come to school with problems nobody would want. They come into the institution adults have created for them and they are sometimes marked as "violent"—their *violent-ness* is a part of their social makeup, how adults read them before they even walk in the door. Many adults seem to have this aspect of the problem well covered, with their zero tolerance, placement committees, and police at the ready. But when addressing "school violence," should we not also be talking about the "school" half of it? What have adults created for the education of young people? How do adults behave in these places? What do adults tell students—through their actions, language, curriculum, policies, structure of the institution—about adult society, about adults' expectations of young people, about what we think of kids?

A POLICY POSTSCRIPT

While I was writing this book, my daughter started kindergarten and her attendance at school was my first experience with schooling as an "insider"—I was now one of the people I would like to interview. At the beginning of the school year I was with a group of parents at my first PTO (Parent Teacher Organization) meeting and my ideas about schooling meshed with my research experiences and called forth some of the themes and reforms raised in this book. Others at the meeting had older children in the school, and these parents exuded a worldliness that I felt lacking in myself. Though we all lived in the better area of the city, the school system was known as one of the worst in the country. The city itself was one of the poorest. In the conversation, one of the parents with a third-grader quipped, "Everything at school just rolls off his shoulders . . . I send him to a prison and he tells me everything is fine." Though this comment was obviously tongue-in-cheek, the rest of the group—including myself—responded with knowing nods of the head. We all knew that for our kids it was not really bad, but for the kids already being considered for retainment, a placement, or a self-contained class it was. We were the lucky in life, and yet still felt the heaviness around us.

Why is it that parents can so easily compare schools to prisons, and what do students learn and how do they react when we send them there? It would be unfair to many hard-working and caring educators to compare all schools or all parts of schooling to an institution as horrible as a prison. But there are aspects of schools, especially in urban areas, that rob some students of their futures and freedom—that resemble prisons organizationally (and sometimes even architecturally). We are at a point in education when it makes little sense to point out, once again, the injustices of some school systems toward primarily urban, poor, and nonwhite students;

rather, it makes more sense to determine when we intend to do something about it and how to begin.

Smaller classes would enable teachers to better supervise students, but as noted earlier, smaller classes (and schools) must accompany the commitment of school staff to take advantage of the change to better know, guide, help, and appreciate the lives of young people. Schools must become centers of intellectual activity, where adults work with students and other adults to develop and improve mind and character, as well as the environment of the school and community, through study, debate, and action. Discipline policy that supports exclusionary forms of punishment and steers kids into the criminal justice system must be done away with. There was a time when the screening committee may have steered poor and minority youth into factory jobs; but now, without the factories, they are steered into ever-expanding prison and "alternative school" systems. When police officers take part in this steering, they add to the fray and neglect.

All manners of reform, including those stated here, must have in common a collaborative effort that would demonstrate to young people that adults are on their side—which is not always the case. Reform requires changes in public policy, popular discourse, and ways of human interaction. We must urge students to act peacefully, but also eliminate all aspects of schooling that ostracize students and maneuver them into life's dead ends. But, again, no one strategy can work alone. Any program or policy must account for the fact that before a violent confrontation happens, the circumstances for the violence are already in place, created by daily experiences, family life, occurrences in schools, relationships between people (youth and police, for example), and in some cases the availability of deadly weapons.

One can only wonder how long individuals in the United States will express shock when confronted with yet another case of school violence. Or for how long we will throw up our hands in bewilderment at the news of another school shooting. Statistics, observations, and even the judgments of people in other countries tell Americans quite clearly and accurately that the United States is a violent nation. It is a leader in rates of youth violence, weapon distribution on both domestic and international markets, political and military violence, violence in the media, and now, it seems, violence in the schools. To be baffled about the causes of school violence is to exercise willful blindness.

References

Adams, D. W. (1988). Fundamental considerations: The deep meaning of native American schooling, 1880–1900. *Harvard Educational Review*, 58, 162–188.

Advancement Project and The Civil Rights Project. (2000). *Opportunities suspended: The devastating consequences of zero tolerance and school discipline policies*. Cambridge: Harvard University.

American Association of University Women Educational Foundation & Louis Harris Associates. (1993). *Hostile hallways: The AAUW survey on sexual harassment in America's schools*. Washington, DC: Author.

Anderson, D. (1998). Curriculum, culture, and community: The challenge of school violence. In M. Tonry & M. Moore (Eds.), *Youth violence* (pp. 317–364). Chicago: University of Chicago Press.

Anderson, E. (1990). Streetwise: Race, class and change in an urban community. Chicago: University of Chicago Press.

Anderson, E. (1997). Violence and the inner-city street code. In J. McCord (Ed.), *Violence and childhood in the inner city* (pp. 1–30). New York: Cambridge University Press.

Anderson, E. (1999). Code of the street: Decency, violence, and the moral life of the inner city. New York: W. W. Norton.

Anyon, J. (1997). *Ghetto schooling: A political economy of urban educational reform*. New York: Teachers College Press.

Apple, M. (1978). Ideology, reproduction, and educational reform. *Comparative Educational Review*, 22(3), 367–387.

Apple, M. (1993). *Official knowledge*. New York: Routledge.

Artz, S. (1998). *Sex, power, and the violent school girl*. Toronto: Trifolium Books.

Athens, L. (1997). *Violent criminal acts and actors revisited*. Urbana and Chicago: University of Illinois Press.

Banfield, E. (1958). *The moral basis of a backward society*. New York: Free Press.

Becker, H. (1963). *Outsiders: Studies in the sociology of deviance*. New York: The Free Press.

Besag, V. E. (1989). *Bullies and victims in schools: A guide to understanding and management*. Milton Keynes and Philadelphia: Open University Press.

Best, J. (1990). *Threatened children: Rhetoric and concern about child-victims*. Chicago: University of Chicago Press.

Biklen, S. (1995). *School work: Gender and the cultural construction of teaching*. New York: Teachers College Press.

Block, A. (1997). *I'm only bleeding: Education as the practice of violence against children*. New York: Peter Lang.

Blumer, H. (1969). *Symbolic interactionism: Perspective and method*. Upper Saddle River, NJ: Prentice-Hall.

Bogdan, R., & Biklen S. K. (1998). *Qualitative research in education: An introduction to theory and practice* (3rd ed.). Boston: Allyn and Bacon.

Bogdan, R., & Taylor, S. (1994). *The social meaning of mental retardation: Two life stories*. New York: Teachers College Press.

Bourdieu, P. (1991). *Language and symbolic power*. Cambridge: Harvard University Press.

Bowles, S., & Gintis, H. (1976). *Schooling in capitalist America: Educational reform and the contradictions of economic life*. New York: Basic Books.

Bureau of Justice Assistance. (1994). *Understanding community policing: A framework for action*. Washington, DC: U.S. Government Printing Office.

Bureau of Municipal Police. (1990). *D.A.R.E.: Senior high school student's handbook*. Criminal Justice Services, New York State: Author.

Bushweller, K. (1993). Guards with guns. *The American School Board Journal*, *180*, 34–37.

Carmichael, P. (1997). Who receives federal Title 1 assistance? Examination of program funding by school poverty rate in New York state. *Educational Evaluation and Policy Analysis*, *19*, 354–359.

Casella, R. (1999). What are we doing when we are "doing" cultural studies in education—and why? *Educational Theory*, *49*, 107–123.

Casella, R. (2000). The benefits of peer mediation in the context of urban conflict and program status. *Urban Education*, *35*, 326–357.

Catalano, R., Arthur, M., Hawkins, D., Berglund, L., & Olsen, J. (1998). Comprehensive community- and school-based interventions to prevent anti-social behavior. In R. Loeber & D. Farrington (Eds.), *Serious and violent juvenile offenders* (pp. 248–283). Thousand Oaks, CA: Sage.

City Chamber of Commerce. (1965). *[Brandon City], New York: The place to set your sites!* [Greater Brandon City]: Chamber of Commerce.

Cloward, R., & Ohlin, L. (1960). *Delinquency and opportunity: A theory of delinquent gangs*. New York: Free Press.

Cousins, L. (1999). "Playing between classes": America's troubles with class, race, and gender in a Black high school and community. *Anthropology and Education Quarterly*, *30*, 294–316.

Davidson, A. L. (1996). *Making and molding identity in schools: Student narratives on race, gender, and academic achievement*. New York: State University of New York Press.

Decker, S., & Van Winkle, B. (1996). *Life in the gang: Family, friends, and violence*. Cambridge: Cambridge University Press.

Denzin, N. (1992). *Symbolic interactionism and cultural studies: The politics of interpretation*. Oxford and Cambridge: Blackwell.

Devine, J. (1996). *Maximum security: The culture of violence in inner-city schools*. Chicago: University of Chicago Press.

Eckert, P. (1989). *Jocks and burnouts: Social categories and identity in the high school*. New York: Teachers College Press.

Elliott, D., Hamburg, B., & Williams, K. (1998). Violence in American schools: An overview. In D. Elliott, B. Hamburg, & K. Williams (Eds.), *Violence in American schools: A new perspective* (pp. 3–30). New York: Cambridge University Press.

Epp, J. R. (1996). Schools, complicity, and sources of violence. In J. R. Epp & A. M. Watkinson (Eds.), *Systemic violence: How schools hurt children* (pp. 1–23). Washington, DC: The Falmer Press.

Erickson, F. (1973). What makes school ethnography "ethnographic"? *Anthropology and Education Quarterly, 4,* 10–19.

Fagan, J., & Wilkinson, D. (1998). Social contexts and functions of adolescent violence. In D. Elliott, B. Hamburg, & K. Williams (Eds.), *Violence in American schools: A new perspective* (pp. 55–93). New York: Cambridge University Press.

Feld, B. (1999). *Bad kids: Race and the transformation of the juvenile court*. New York: Oxford University Press.

Feuerverger, G. (1998). Neve Shalom/Wahat Al-Salam: A Jewish-Arab school for peace. *Teachers College Record, 99,* 692–730.

Fine, M. (1991). *Framing dropouts: Notes on the politics of an urban public high school*. Albany: State University of New York Press.

Fishman, S. (1979). The double-vision of education in the nineteenth-century: The romantic and the grotesque. In B. Finkelstein (Ed.), *Regulated children/liberated children: Education in psychohistorical perspective*. New York: Psychohistory Press.

Foley, D. (1990). *Learning capitalist culture*. Philadelphia: University of Pennsylvania Press.

Fordham, S. (1993). "Those loud black girls": (Black) women, silence and gender "passing" in the academy. *Anthropology and Education Quarterly, 24,* 3–32.

Fordham, S. (1996). *Blacked out: Dilemmas of race, identity, and success at Capital High*. Chicago: University of Chicago Press.

Foucault, M. (1980). *Power/knowledge: Selected interviews and other writings*. New York: Pantheon Books.

Foucault, M. (1995). *Discipline and punish: The birth of the prison*. New York: Vintage Books. (Original work published 1975)

Fowler, G. (1969). *The first 120 years: An historical narrative of the [Brandon city] public schools*. New York: [Brandon] City School District.

Freire, P. (1970). *Pedagogy of the oppressed*. New York: Continuum Publishing.

Friend, R. (1998). Heterosexism, homophobia, and the culture of schooling. In S. Books (Ed.), *Invisible children in the society and its schools* (pp. 137–166). Mahwah, NJ: Lawrence Erlbaum.

Fuentes, A. (1998). The crackdown on kids. *The Nation, 15*(22), 20–22.

Garbarino, J. (1999). *Lost boys: Why our sons turn violent and how we can save them*. New York: Free Press.

Gellert, G. A. (1997). *Confronting violence: Answers to questions about the epi-*

demic destroying American's homes and communities. New York: Westview Press.

Giroux, H. (1983). *Theory and resistance in education.* South Hadley, MA: Bergin and Garvey.

Goffman, E. (1963). *Stigma: Notes on the management of spoiled identity.* New York: Simon and Schuster, Inc.

Goldstein, A. (1994). *The ecology of aggression.* New York and London: Plenum Press.

Goldstein, A., Harootunian, B., & Conoley, J. C. (1994). *Student aggression: Prevention, management, and replacement training.* New York: The Guilford Press.

Gottfredson, G., & Gottfredson, D. (1985). *Victimization in school.* New York and London: Plenum Press.

Grant, G. (1988). *The world we created at Hamilton High.* Cambridge: Harvard University Press.

Guerra, N. (1997). Intervening to prevent childhood aggression in the inner city. In J. McCord (Ed.), *Violence and childhood in the inner city* (pp. 256–312). New York: Cambridge University Press.

Guetzloe, E. C. (1989). *Youth suicide: What the educator should know.* Arlington, VA: The Council for Exceptional Children.

Hafen, B. Q., & Frandsen, K. J. (1986). *Youth suicide: Depression and loneliness.* Evergreen, CO: Cordillera Press Inc.

Harrington, M. (1962). *The other America.* New York: Macmillan.

Hearing on school violence before the Subcommittee on Elementary, Secondary, and Vocational Education of the Committee on Education and Labor. (1994). House of Representatives, One Hundred and Third Congress, Second Session, Washington, DC.

Herbert, S. (1998). Police subculture reconsidered. *Criminology, 36,* 343–369.

Holmes, T., & Murrell, J. (1995). Schools, discipline, and the uniformed police officer. *NASSP Bulletin, 79,* 60–64.

Howell, J. (1998). Promising programs for youth gang violence prevention and intervention. In R. Loeber & D. Farrington (Eds.), *Serious and violent juvenile offenders* (pp. 284–312). Thousand Oaks, CA: Sage.

Hylton, J. (1996). Know-how. *The American School Board Journal, 183,* 45–46.

Hyman, I., & Snook, P. (1999). *Dangerous schools.* San Francisco: Jossey-Bass.

Juvenile Justice Commission (1996, May). *Report on Juvenile Crime.* Albany, NY: State of New York Department of Law.

Kappeler, V., Sluder, R., & Alpert, G. (1994). *Forces of deviance: Understanding the dark side of policing.* Prospect Heights, IL: Waveland Press.

Katz, J. (1995). Reconstructing masculinity in the locker room: The mentors in violence prevention project. *Harvard Educational Review, 65,* 163–188.

Katz, M. (1989). *The undeserving poor: From the war on poverty to the war on welfare.* New York: Pantheon Books.

Kelling, G., & Coles, C. (1998). *Fixing broken windows: Restoring order and reducing crime in our communities.* New York: Free Press.

Kivel, P. (1999). *Boys will be men: Raising our sons for courage, caring, and community.* Gabriola Island, BC: New Society Publishers.

Kochis, D. (1995). The effectiveness of project DARE: Does it work? *Journal of Alcohol and Drug Education, 40,* 40–47.

Lawrence, R. (1998). *School crime and juvenile justice.* New York: Oxford University Press.

Lesko, N. (1996). Past, present, and future conceptions of adolescence. *Educational Theory, 46,* 453–472.

Levinson, B. A., & Holland, D. C. (1996). The cultural production of the educated person: An introduction. In B. Levinson, D. Foley, & D. Holland (Eds.), *The cultural production of the educated person: Critical ethnographies of schooling and local practice* (pp. 1–54). Albany: State University of New York Press.

Lewis, O. (1961). *The children of Sanchez.* New York: Random House.

Liebow, E. (1967). *Tally's corner: A study of Negro streetcorner men.* New York: Little, Brown and Company.

Lincoln, Y. (1988). Do inquiry paradigms imply inquiry methodologies? In D. Fetterman (Ed.), *Qualitative approaches to evaluation in education* (pp. 89–115). New York: Praeger.

MacDonald, I. M. (1996). Expanding the lens: Student perceptions of school violence. In J. Epp & A. Watkinson (Eds.), *Systemic violence: How schools hurt children* (pp. 83–92). Washington, DC: The Falmer Press.

Marans, S., & Schaefer, M. (1998). Community policing, schools, and mental health: The challenge of collaboration. In D. Elliott, B. Hamburg, & K. Williams (Eds.), *Violence in American schools: A new perspective* (pp. 312–347). New York: Cambridge University Press.

Marcus, E. (1996). *Why suicide?* New York: HarperCollins Publishers Inc.

McCord, J. (1997). Placing American urban violence in context. In J. McCord (Ed.), *Violence and childhood in the inner city* (pp. 78–115). New York: Cambridge University Press.

McQuillan, P. (1998). *Educational opportunity in an urban American high school: A cultural analysis.* Albany: State University of New York Press.

Miller, J. (1998). *Last one over the wall: The Massachusetts experiment in closing reform schools.* Columbus: Ohio State University Press.

Moynihan, D. (1965). *The Negro family: The case for national action.* Washington, DC: Office of Policy Planning and Research, U.S. Department of Labor.

National Center for Education Statistics. (1995). *Gangs and victimization at school.* Washington, DC: U.S. Department of Education.

National Center for Education Statistics. (1998). *Indicators of school crime and safety.* Washington, DC: U.S. Department of Education.

National Commission on Excellence in Education. (1983). *A nation at risk: The imperative for educational reform.* Washington, DC: U.S. Government Printing Office.

National Governors' Association and President's Education Summit. (1991). *America 2000: An education strategy.* Washington, DC: U.S. Government Printing Office.

National Institute of Education. (1977). *Violent schools—safe schools: The safe school study report to Congress.* Washington, DC: U.S. Department of Health, Education, and Welfare.

National Institute of Justice. (1995). *Youth violence, guns, and illicit drug markets.* Washington, DC: U.S. Department of Justice.

Neiderhoffer, A. (1967). *Behind the shield: The police in urban society.* New York: Doubleday.

Noddings, N. (1992). *The challenge to care in schools: An alternative approach to education.* New York: Teachers College Press.

Noddings, N. (1996). Learning to care and be cared for. In A. M. Hoffman (Ed.), *Schools, violence, and society* (pp. 185–198). Westport, CT: Praeger.

Noguera, P. A. (1995). Preventing and producing violence: A critical analysis of responses to school violence. *Harvard Educational Review, 65,* 189–212.

Oakes, J. (1995). Two cities' tracking and within-school segregation. *Teachers College Record, 96,* 681–690.

O'Neill, A. (1988). *Syracuse: The heart of New York.* Northridge, CA: Windsor Publications.

Pattillo-McCoy, M. (1999). *Black picket fences: Privilege and peril among the black middle class.* Chicago: University of Chicago Press.

Perkinson, H. (1995). *The imperfect panacea: American faith in education.* New York: McGraw-Hill.

Perlstein, D. (1998). Saying the unsaid: Girl killing and the curriculum. *Journal of Curriculum and Supervision, 14,* 88–104.

Petersen, G., Pietrzak, D., & Speaker, K. (1998). The enemy within: A national study on school violence and prevention. *Urban Education, 33,* 331–359.

Peterson, P. (1983). Urban politics and changing schools: A competitive view. In R. K. Goodenow & D. Ravitch (Eds.), *Schools in cities: Consensus and conflict in American educational history* (pp. 223–248). New York: Holmes & Meier.

Pinderhughes, H. (1997). *Race in the hood: Conflict and violence among urban youth.* Minneapolis: University of Minnesota Press.

Pitch, T. (1995) *Limited responsibilities: Social movements and criminal justice.* New York: Routledge.

Pollack, W. (1999). *Real boys: Rescuing our sons from the myths of boyhood.* New York: Henry Holt & Co.

Prothrow-Stith, D. (1991). *Deadly consequences: How violence is destroying our teenage population and a plan to begin solving the problem.* New York: HarperCollins Publishers.

Public Law 99-570. (1986). *Drug-Free Schools and Communities Act of 1986,* 20 USC 4601.

Public Law 101-647. (1990). *Crime Control Act of 1990.* 18 USC 1.

Public Law 101-647 SEC 1702. (1990). *Gun-Free School Zones Act.* 18 USC 921.

Public Law 103-227 SEC 701. (1994). *Safe Schools Act.* 20 USC 5961.

Public Law 103-227 SEC 1031. (1994). *Gun-Free Schools Act.* 20 USC 2701.

Public Law 103-227 [H.R. 1804]. (1994). *Goals 2000: Educate America Act.* 20 USC 5801.

Public Law 103-382. (1994). *Safe and Drug-Free Schools and Communities Act.* SEC 4001, 20 USC 7101.

Public Law 105-302. (1998). Amendment to the *Omnibus Crime Control and Safe Streets Act of 1968,* SEC 1, 42 USC 2796dd.

Ravitch, D., & Viteritti, J. (1997). New York: The obsolete factory. In D. Ravitch & J. Viteritti (Eds.), *New schools for a new century: The redesign of urban education* (pp. 17–36). New Haven: Yale University Press.

Riessman, F. (1962). *The culturally deprived child.* New York: Harper and Row.

Rist, R. (1970). Student social class and teacher expectations: The self-fulfilling prophecy in ghetto education. *Harvard Educational Review, 40,* 411–451.

Roman, L. (1993). White is a color! White defensiveness, postmodernism, and anti-racist pedagogy. In C. McCarthy & W. Crichlow (Eds.), *Race, identity and representation in education* (pp. 71–88). New York: Routledge.

Sampson, R. J. (1997). The embeddedness of child and adolescent development: A community-level perspective on urban violence. In J. McCord (Ed.), *Violence and childhood in the inner city* (pp. 31–77). New York: Cambridge University Press.

Shaw, C. (1966). *The jack-roller: A delinquent boy's own story.* Chicago: University of Chicago Press. (Original work published 1930)

Short, J. F. (1997). *Poverty, ethnicity, and violent crime.* Boulder: Westview.

Sikes, G. (1997). *8 ball chicks: A year in the violent world of girl gangs.* New York: Dell Publishing Group, Inc.

Sinclair, B. (1999). Report on State implementation of the Gun-Free Schools Act: Final report, August 1999. Washington, DC: U.S. Department of Education, Office of Elementary and Secondary Education and Planning and Evaluation Service.

Skelly, M. (1997). The school beat. *The American School Board Journal, 184,* 25–27.

Smith, S. (1996). Saving our cities from the experts. In W. Ayers & P. Ford (Eds.), *City kids, city teachers: Reports from the front row* (pp. 91–109). New York: The New Press.

Soriano, M., Soriano, F., & Jimenez, E. (1994). School violence among culturally diverse populations: Sociocultural and institutional considerations. *School Psychology Review, 23,* 216–235.

Steet, L. (1998). Traditional stories of female students in an alternative school. In S. Books (Ed.), *Invisible children in the society and its schools* (pp. 111–120). Mahwah, NJ: Lawrence Erlbaum.

Stein, N. (1995). Sexual harassment in school: The public performance of gendered violence. *Harvard Educational Review, 65,* 145–188.

Stein, N. (1999). *Classrooms and courtrooms: Facing sexual harassment in K–12 schools.* New York: Teachers College Press.

Terry, W. (1985). *Policing society: An occupational view.* New York: John Wiley & Sons.

Thrasher, F. (1927). *The gang: A study of 1,313 gangs in Chicago.* Chicago: University of Chicago Press.

Toby, J. (1994). The politics of school violence. *Public Interest, 116,* 34–56.

Tonry, M. (1995). *Malign neglect: Race, crime, and punishment in America.* New York: Oxford University Press.

Tucker, J., Marx, J., & Long, L. (1998). "Moving on": Residential mobility and children's school lives. *Sociology of Education, 71,* 111–129.

Tyack, D., & Cuban, L. (1995). *Tinkering toward utopia: A century of public school reform*. Cambridge: Harvard University Press.

Tyack, D. B. (1974). *The one best system: A history of American urban education*. Cambridge: Harvard University Press.

U.S. Bureau of the Census. (1990). *Census of population and housing*. Washington, DC: Author.

Van Maanen, J. (1973). Observations on the making of policemen. *Human Organization, 32*, 407–418.

Vigil, J. D. (1999). Streets and schools: How educators can help Chicano marginalized gang youth. *Harvard Educational Review, 69*, 270–288.

Vinovskis, M. (1996). An analysis of the concept and uses of systemic educational reform. *American Educational Research Journal, 33*, 53–85.

Waldner-Haugrud, L. (1995). Sexual coercion on dates: It's not just rape. *Update on Law Related Education, 19*, 15–18.

Ward, J. V. (1995). Cultivating a morality of care in African American adolescents: A culture-based model of violence prevention. *Harvard Educational Review, 65*, 175–188.

Warner, B., Weist, M., & Krulak, A. (1999). Risk factors for school violence. *Urban Education, 34*, 52–68.

Watkinson, A. M. (1996). Suffer the little children who come into schools. In J. R. Epp & A. M. Watkinson (Eds.), *Systemic violence: How schools hurt children* (pp. 173–190). Washington, DC: The Falmer Press.

Weinberg, A., & Weinberg, L. (1964). *The muckrakers*. New York: Capricorn Books.

Weitzer, R., & Tuch, S. (1999). Race, class, and perceptions of discrimination by the police. *Crime and Delinquency, 45*, 494–505.

Willis, P. (1977). *Learning to labor: How working class kids get working class jobs*. New York: Columbia University Press.

Yarmey, A. (1990). *Understanding police and police work: Psychosocial issues*. New York: New York University Press.

Zagumny, M., & Thompson, M. (1997). Does D.A.R.E. work? An evaluation in rural Tennessee. *Journal of Alcohol and Drug Education, 42*, 32–41.

Index

About the Author

Ronnie Casella is an assistant professor of secondary education and educational foundations at Central Connecticut State University. He has taught high school in Colombia, South America, and college-level courses at a number of urban universities. He is the author of *At Zero Tolerance: Punishment, Prevention, and School Violence*, as well as articles that have appeared in *Urban Education*, *Anthropology and Education Quarterly*, *Educational Theory*, and numerous other journals. His research for this book was undertaken while he was a research associate for the Violence Prevention Project at Syracuse University and for the Hamilton Fish National Institute on School and Community Violence at George Washington University. His current research involves a case study of a city high school social worker and the structuring of schooling for students determined to be socially and emotionally disturbed (SED).